# ENCYCLOPEDIA
# CORRUPTION
# IN THE WORLD

Book 2: Corruption - a Political Perspective

## JUDIVAN J. VIEIRA

authorHOUSE®

*AuthorHouse™*
*1663 Liberty Drive*
*Bloomington, IN 47403*
*www.authorhouse.com*
*Phone: 1 (800) 839-8640*

*Published by AuthorHouse 04/17/2018*

*ISBN: 978-1-5462-3290-2 (sc)*
*ISBN: 978-1-5462-3288-9 (hc)*
*ISBN: 978-1-5462-3289-6 (e)*

*Library of Congress Control Number: 2018904219*

*Print information available on the last page.*

# ACHOWLEDGMENTS

To:

God.

My mother *(in memoriam)* who when I was still a construction labor told me that studying would be the turning point in my life.
Eliane Caetano, my personal assistant and office manager, for the effectiveness and help during the research process and bibliographic organization, for the seven years that made this work a scientific reality and innovative project.

*"Thus, to the unjust and intemperate man, it was possible, from the beginning, not to be unjust and intemperate; on which account they are voluntarily so; but when they are become such characters, it is no longer possible for them not to be so; as neither is it possible for him who has thrown a stone, to resume it; at the same time it was in his power to emit from his hand and hurl the stone; for he contained the principle of action in himself."*

*Aristotle*

# CONTENTS

## BOOK II
*Corruption - a Political Perspective*

# PRESENTATION

Arke - Art Representation & Projects, has the honor to introduce you to the First Encyclopedia about Corruption In the World, written by PHD Judivan J Vieira.

Corruption has been such a very important subject all over the world and its importance has been increasing at each blink of eye. There's no society on the world surface that have not tried - at least once in a life time - the taste of it, as a way to handle its own political and economic daily struggles. From the top to the bottom of our globe - and who knows if not beyond – crimes such bribery, exploitation, extortion, fraud, graft, malfeasance and other endless number of illegal practices, have been illustrating some important daily headlines in the most important newspapers out and about.

The use and misuse of this perennial word, which register goes back in times of our history as an unsolved problem, however, has much more in store than we can supposedly wonder. Not even the concept of celestial paradise, the imaginary of perfection capable of bringing the deepest supernatural feeling to all believer human on earth could keep itself out of it.

But, why to talk about corruption? What is corruption indeed? Who's the corrupt and what's its social, political and economic profile? What's the oldest roster in history about it? How history has framed it and how politics have taken their piece of this huge cake artistically decorated with felonious ingredients?

In the attempt to answer all these questions and so many more, Brazilian writer and an intellectual by excellence, Professor Dr Judivan Vieira comes to the table to feed us with such insatiable literary banquet. First published in 2014 in Portuguese, The First Encyclopedia about Corruption in the World brought a new perspective on how to frame the subject, getting away with casuistry by bringing the accuracy of philosophical questions that lead to a better understanding of it, as a selective topic that never ends. From the religious inferences to the contemporary conceptions, the 5 books evolve according to our needs to look at the main plot as a big and complex landscape, having the permission to be persuaded by a profound 101conversation between the author and his reader.

The first book, Corruption - a historical perspective, give us the tools we all need to start a long and intriguing journey towards a world which reveals itself as the face of an old plague, always reinventing itself to fit the historical gaps between now and then. Followed by book two, Corruption - a political perspective, the author digs deep into the world most outstanding theories, exposing philosophers, economists, politicians and all sort of elements that can orchestrate a more comprehensive analysis about the State and its functioning, and Democracy and its main role in this context. Moving on with three other books to complete his magnificent work, professor Vieira uses all his experience as a Federal Prosecutor working with Brazilian Government, to master his audience, showing a remarkable knowledge of his work environment. Legal Perspective of Corruption, International Law Perspective on corruption and Last but not least, Anti-corruption tools in Mercosur and around the world.

We hope all the issues registered, exposed and discussed along these pages – carefully prepared to unveil new perspectives on our thoughts about the theme - can lead you to clarification and a fair attitude before such important matter. Enjoy it!

Joao S Brandao Junior, Arke- Art Representation & Projects's curator

# INTRODUCTION

Francisco Heidemann and José Francisco Salm (2010: 123), in writing about the theory of the public choice and about politics as a collective deliberation of individuals driven by their own interess, state that *"The interests of politicians and bureaucrats are distinct from the interests of voters."*

Fortini Cristiana (2008: 363), when addressing the primary and secondary public interest in public policies, says:

> "It is also convenient to investigate the extent to which the public interest is not confused in practice with the interest of the administrator who, fleetingly, finds himself in the exercise of power. How far does the statement - primary public interest as a collective interest – find meaning as something that must be enforced and not as part of the common sense?"

Michael Alexandrovich Bakunin (2006: 106), in turn, suspicious of the honesty of politics, was categorical when he said:

> "The same can be said of politics, which can be summed up by the following rule: 'it is necessary to subdue and despoil the people in such a way that it does not complain much about its fate, that it does not forget to subjugate, and that it does not have time to think about resistance and revolt."

Tomas Moro (2003:55) had no doubt in saying that:

> "Todo rey es una suerte de fuente de la cual fluye una
> lluvia constante de beneficios o daños que cae sobre toda
> la población."

Voltaire (1993:60-61), convinced that even philosophers are corrupt,
said:

> "Sabéis, Señor, cómo Bacon fue acusado de un crimen
> que no es muy propio de un filósofo, de haberse dejado
> corromper por dinero; sabéis cómo fue condenado por la
> Cámara de los Pares a una multa de cerca de cuatrocientas
> mil libras de nuestra moneda, a perder su dignidad de
> Canciller y de Par."

It is impossible to ignore that the pledge for a "better tomorrow" to
wrap politics and that corruption continues to reduce this truth only to
some social classes in detriment of the overwhelming majority of voters.
Worse still, it is to imagine that the public officer, the guardian elected to
protect the treasury, is the one who plunders it.

# CHAPTER 1

# The Quest for The Perfect State

Writing about politics presupposes a minimum of understanding of two philosophical thoughts. One is the Platonic-Augustinian in which Quentin Skinner (1996: 70-71) asserts *that the political society is seen as an order determined by God and imposed upon fallen men as a remedy for their sins.* Another is the Aristotelian-Thomistic thought, *which treats the polis as a purely human creation destined to serve worldly ends.* In the latter case, politics is an art of government of men over men.

Skinner (1996:70-71), analyzing the Platonic-Augustinian ideology and the Aristotelian-Thomistic pragmatism on political life, says:

> "In Augustine, the theory of political society is subordinated to an eschatology, which considers the life of the pilgrim on Earth little more than a preparation for the life to come. Aristotle, on the other hand, says in Book I of Politics that the art of 'living and living well' in the *polis* is a self-sufficient ideal, which does not need any further purpose to acquire its full meaning "(pp. 9-13).

The second book of this collection is about this art of governing, associated with the infallible Aristotelian logic that *if each one follows his only individual will, the government of human lives will be destroyed and totally dissolved*, an idea that will be defended by David Hume more than 20 centuries later, as Skinner explains (1996: 65-66):

1

"... how to achieve such unity between the interests of the city and those of its citizens as individuals. To this question, the authors we are considering propose a response that, once developed by the Italian Renaissance humanists, would provide the foundation for one of the greatest intellectual traditions of analysis of virtue and corruption in civic life. We can say that in the evolution of the modern political theory there were two main lines of approach of this theme. One of them says that government will be effective whenever its institutions are strong and corrupt whenever its machinery fails to function properly. The great exponent of this conception is Hume. The other line of thought, on the contrary, believes that if the men who control government institutions are corrupt, the best possible institutions will not be able to mold or restrain them, whereas, if they are virtuous, the quality of institutions will become a topic of importance. This tradition, of which Machiavelli and Montesquieu are the greatest representatives, defends that it is not so much the machinery of government but the spirit of rulers, of the people, and of the laws that most need to be defended...."

The Renaissance civic humanists of the sixteenth century, and also the writers who at the time wrote to instruct city magistrates, as Skinner recalled (1996: 155), had the firmest certainty that in defense of liberty and justice lay the supreme values of political life

Machiavelli vehemently fought civic humanism by saying that the prince who acts virtuously in all cases will soon discover how much he will suffer among so many who are not virtuous. Moreover, he advises that the prince should have as a priority to preserve his state and only then consider the goals of honor, glory, and fame.

In this historical path, politics continues to weave the contours of the State that, after the Lutheran reform, will gain anthropocentric strength insofar as it slowly "moves away from God" and becomes a secular entity.

This change will be the cradle of the Modern State as we know it today because its perspective is now mankind and the least happiness to which it is entitled as part of the *polis*, for if this is the body, the exterior of the social covering, its content is the man without which the *polis* makes as much sense as a ghost town.

The humanist man is mainly under the sign of a god or a Nature that creates all things. Such a man could not be expected to have his living detached from his deities unless his eyes were opened by scientific principles, as it happened when he began to observe his environment and see that the leaves fall from the trees according to natural laws and not by the breath of God.

This perspective, that is no longer only vertical in search of God above all things, becomes horizontal, and man is gradually presented to his own anthropocentric image reflected in the mirror of life.

This image of oneself on the polished surface of existence, will teach that it is possible to live with divine laws, natural laws, and human laws, a vision that has become cultivated by the pre-Socratic philosophers, such as those of Thales of Miletus.

Maturing requires time and experience. The path of historical learning was long and in it, man built cities, empires, monarchies, and republics, consulting his oracles, or, under religious foundations of implacable gods, warriors, and avengers, who at times were capable of gestures of mercy with his creation.

The principle of legality was imposed together with the idea of the gods and their governments over men, in which breaking their commandments is a cause whose effect is physical and spiritual punishment.

These conceptions were exacerbated in Christianity and, on them, Skinner (1996: 367) states:

> "...it was during the revolution of the 1530s that the theoretical basis for the policy of separation of State and Church was established that almost two centuries later would be officially advocated by the Whig oligarchy, then in power, to be endorsed by ecclesiastical exponents of Lockean liberalism, like Benjamin Hoadly..."

The Lutheran Protestant doctrine was embraced by important bishops and theologians of the time, like Jacques-Benigne Bossuet, who in the seventeenth century devoted his main political work (Politics taken from the very words of the Holy Scriptures), to the heir of Louis XIV, in which he affirms that the power of the king must extend to the judgment of all

3

the causes, ecclesiastical or not, and that this power must be absolute, for *there is no one to whom the king ought to be accountable for* (pp. 92-4), an idea resultant from the absolutist understanding similar to the one that defends that *the king can do no wrong.*

The State and religion have always fought for power. They did it either by the power of empire, or sometimes trying to strengthen it based on the support of the people, offering social welfare as exchange currency. However, despite the evolution of State secularism, it is naive to think that the State overcame the church in mercy or social justice. Both pursue power for power.

The democratic state, in the modern version, will be constituted from all the evolutions and revolutions for which the government has been passing over time, but mainly by the foundations of constitutionalism from the sixteenth century onwards. On this genesis of the modern State Skinner points out (p. 426):

"The fundamental step given by the Thomists in discussing the concept of political society was to retake the Aquinas conception of a universe governed by a hierarchy of laws. First, they have placed the eternal law (*lex aeterna*) by which God himself acts. Next, comes the divine law (*lex divina*) that God reveals directly to men in the Scriptures and on which the Church was founded. It follows the law of nature (*lex naturalis*, sometimes called *ius naturale*), which God 'implants' in men, so that they may be able to understand His designs and intentions for the world. And finally, there is the positive human law, also called *human lex*, *lex civilis* or *postivum*, which men create and promulgate for themselves in order to govern the republics they establish."

Saint Thomas Aquinas elaborated his philosophical-political thinking on the basis of the ideas of Thales of Miletus and, above all, of Aristotle, as it appears of his elaboration on the three characteristics of the natural condition of mankind.

Skinner (1996: 435) notes that, according to Aquinas, the natural condition of mankind:

1) involves a natural community;
2) is governed by the law of nature; and
3) is based on the recognition of freedom, equality, and natural independence of all members.

In addressing the resurgence of Thomism and its theory of political society, civil government, and the need for laws to protect it, Skinner (qt. 434, 437-438) observes that the political society exists because its principles were already present in the heart of man. This is how he points it out:

"It means that it is impossible for any man, under any conditions, to 'somehow ignore his primary principles.' Consequently, even before the establishment of the political society, the dictates of that law would already be fully present 'in the hearts of men'.

(...)

They specifically criticize the Stoic thesis - defended by Cicero and endorsed by numerous humanists - that before civil societies were formed, men would have begun their lives as lonely wanderers. They, therefore, insist on the typical Thomistic axiom according to which, as Victoria explains in The Civil Power, 'it is indeed essential for man to never live alone.'

(...)

Although the precepts of morality have been 'inscribed in our hearts,' as Molina affirms, 'it is nevertheless easy, especially in the face of the loss of our innocence, ignoring many aspects of morality and feeling uncertainty over many others' (p. 1705). The consequence, says Suárez in his dissertation on the 'need for laws,' is that 'peace and justice can never be maintained without proper laws,' for 'the common man has difficulty understanding what is necessary for the general well-being, and almost never strives to get it himself.'

(...)

We can now see, as Molina and Suarez argue, what compels men to give up their natural freedom in favor of the impositions of positive law: this decision is indirectly motivated, of course, by self-interest. We have come to realize that unless we introduce some regulatory mechanism into our lives to ensure that the dictates of the laws of nature are duly observed, we can not expect to live decently and safely. As Suárez says, our natural condition is such that 'each individual in particular will be concerned only with his own advantages, which will often be contrary to the general well being.' This makes it 'preferable' to exchange this condition for another, more structured, 'simply in view of our well-being.'

(...)

Suárez endorses this analysis later, when discussing the completely different thesis of Victoria. The latter denies that an institution as perfect as a political society could be erected on irregular foundations, like our mutual selfish calculations. Examining the question in his *On Civil Power*, he accepts that the essential reason for establishing a republic is that 'no society can continue to hold itself without some strength and power to govern and provide it', for 'if all men would remain equal and no one would ever be subjected to any power, each individual would only follow his/her own desires and seek own pleasure, in totally different directions,' and consequently 'society would necessarily fall apart.

These Aristotelian-Thomistic pillars will support the Enlightenment of the seventeenth and eighteenth centuries, and it is in this anthropocentric period that the seeds of the Modern State will flourish and bear fruit, with the idea being reinforced in the last centuries, that *in the nature of things, the power to organize the republic resides immediately in the community*, as Skinner defends (qt. pp. 439).

The same author also says (qt. pp. 459-460) that:

"According to Suárez, the act performed by a free people by instituting a ruler must be interpreted - as Grotius and especially Hobbes later discussed - not only as an act of transference but also as an abrogation of his original sovereignty. On an ideological level, the importance of this idea was to adapt to the theory of the fundamental state in natural law, with an emphasis on the original freedom of the people... On the intellectual perspective, a no less important consequence was the establishment of the vocabulary of concepts and a corresponding style of political argument that Grotius, Hobbes, Pufendorf, and their successors adopted and developed by building, in the course of the following century, the classical version of the theory of State based on natural law."

Skinner's conclusion (qt. pp. 620-21) on the meaning of the word State, as we know it today, is as follows:

"... the Latin term *status* had already been used by legal and scholastic writers in the late Middle Ages in various political contexts. But even if in these cases we think it is correct to translate *status* as a state - a choice that perhaps some historians of the medieval period tend to assume too easily – it is clearly something very different from the modern idea of the state. Before the sixteenth century, the term status only appeared in the words of political thinkers to refer to: the state or condition in which a ruler (*status principis*) is found, or in a more general sense the state of the nation, this is the condition of the kingdom as a whole (*status regni*). Both of these meanings lack the typically modern idea of the state as a form of public power separate from the ruler and the ruled, constituting the supreme political authority within a defined territory."

The forces of history, politics, canon law, and civil law unite to engineer, from the Middle Ages on, the liberal idea that will settle intellectually in the sixteenth and seventeenth centuries and become a spatial and temporal reality from the American Revolution (1776) and the French Revolution (1789).

The liberal State will be born under the sign of the promise of equality, freedom, and fraternity among men, and will gradually settle down as a democracy of promises, translated into our present democratic states.

The paternity of liberal theory is attributed to Adam Smith who in his book, *The Wealth of Nations* (composed of five volumes published in March 1776, in London) defends the foundations, objectives, and principles that govern the current democratic states.

If you analyze articles 1 to 4 of the Brazilian Constitution of October 5, 1988, abstracting from the political aspects and focusing on the economic ones, you will find the Smithian liberal principles.

Carefully read the following passage of the Brazilian Constitution and then compare it with the description of Smith's thought that we present below:

"Article 1 - The Federative Republic of Brazil, formed by the indissoluble union of States and Counties, as well as the Federal District, is a Democratic State of Law founded upon:

I.    sovereignty;
II.   citizenship;
III.  human dignity;
IV.   social values of work and free initiative;
V.    political pluralism.
       (...)

Article 3 - The fundamental objectives of the Federative Republic of Brazil are:

I.    to build a free, just and unified society;

II.    to guarantee national development;

III.    to eradicate poverty and substandard living conditions and to reduce social and regional inequalities;

IV.    to promote the well-being of all, without prejudice as to origin, race, sex, color, age and any other forms of discrimination.

Article 4 - The international relations of the Federative Republic of Brazil are governed by the following principles:

I.    national independence;

II.    prevalence of human rights;

III.    self-determination of peoples;

IV.    non-intervention;

V.    equality among States;

VI.    defense of peace;

VII.    peaceful solution of conflicts;

VIII.    repudiation of terrorism and racism;

IX.    cooperation among people for the progress of humanity;

X.    concession of political asylum."

In the book collection *Colección Grandes Pensadores* (pages 121-125) the following clarifications on the thinking of the "father of the economy" are recorded:

1 - in the first book, he discusses what wealth consists of, what produces it, and how it is distributed among the population;

2 - in the second book, he talks about the nature, accumulation, and the use of capital;

3 - in the third book, he analyzes the different economic policies implemented by different governments, as well as the actual functioning of the principles about wealth, presented in Books 1 and 2;

4 - in the fourth book, he analyzes the theories with which he contrasts the nature and the causes of wealth. He names his theory as the *system of natural liberty*; and

5 - in the last book, he deals with the revenues of public money, the functions of the State, and of the public expenses.

For Smith, *la sociedad civilizada se caracteriza porque tiene un gobierno y porque hay en ella desigualdade de clases, pero tambíén porque hay mucha división del trabajo.*

He makes it clear that inequality is the key that opens the door to development because it asserts that the clearest circumstance on which progress depends on is the division of labor and the extent of the market.

The extent of the market to which he refers to is directly linked to the size of the population and to the security and ease of the means of communication, which is why the progress of commerce is always linked to the wealth produced by the Nation, that is why he asserts that *en las sociedades de cazadores existe mucha igualdad, y todos trabajan, pero hay muy poco comercio. La consecuencia es que son pobres* (ob. cit. p. 124).

As much as his economic theory has been and still is the subject of criticism, it is the one that has unleashed the knot of the state's political-economic relations.

As we see it, Smith's theory can be schematized as follows:

GOVERNMENT

SOCIAL INEQUALITY

LABOR DIVISION

DEVELOPMENT

In approaching the political class and its relation to the public assets, Smith is categorical in calling it a rogue and an astute animal, whose advice is guided by the momentary fluctuations of the market. Here is what he states (see pp. 139-140):

"La hacienda pública. De lo que se trata en la hacienda pública es de que los impuestos perjudiquen lo mínimo el incremento conjunto de la riqueza y de la división del trabajo. Ello sólo puede hacerse si se conoce bien su naturaleza y causas. No es una buena tarea para «la habilidad de ese animal astuto y ladino que se llama político, cuyos consejos se orientan por las fluctuaciones momentáneas de los negocios» Por el contrario, es la tarea más compleja de una ciencia del legislador, la más necesitada de cono cimiento experto."

One of the pillars of the liberal Smithian State is democracy. Noam Chomsky (2008 pp. 44, 64), in his analysis of the vices of democracy, says that the threat comes not from over-management but from its absence, and further warns:

"God - the Communist commentators to the contrary - is clearly democratic. He distributes brain power universally, but He quite justifiably expects us to do something efficient and constructive with that priceless gift. That is what management is all about. Its medium is human capacity, and its most fundamental task is to deal with change. It is the gate through which social, political, economic, technological change, indeed change in every dimension, is rationally spread through society.

(…) the real threat to democracy comes not from over management, but from under management. To undermanage reality is not to keep it free. It is simply to let some force other than reason shape reality (…) if it is not reason that rules man, then man falls short of his potential.

(…)

Thomas Jefferson warned that when citizens 'become inattentive to public affairs,'the government 'turns itself into a pack.'"

René Passet (2002:11) says that *A world dies, and another tries very hard to be born.*

Many were the forms of states devoured by time. Finally, the liberal State has given way to the neoliberal and this will give way to other forms because there is no concealment that time will not wear.

I completely support Passet when he says that man is the measure of all things. This way of thinking embraces both the creationist and the evolutionary theory because cognoscence itself demonstrates that for man there are all things and that the end of evolution is to cover him with ethical and moral consciousness.

This is the reflection of René Passet (pp. 32, 35, 83):

"The creative destruction

I.   'Man, the measure of all things'

Nature does not appear in the forms that allow it to directly satisfy the needs of men. His resources, said Henri Guitton, 'are too numerous or insufficiently numerous; they are not in the ideal place nor in the ideal time, in the desired moment; they do not have the desired form [...]. The economic activity is, thus, the form of human activity through which men struggle to reduce nature's maladjustment to their needs.' More laconic, Henri Laborit mentioned that it is not enough for us to feed ourselves, to open our mouths towards the solar photons, from which all food ultimately comes to us.

(...)

Efficacy, by definition, is 'what produces the expected effect' (Larousse). The performance of a system can only be defined, therefore, by the degree of achievement of the purpose to which it should serve. What can, then, the measure of economic performance regardless of its human ends mean?

(...)

'Beyond this level, with the capitalist base being constituted and essential needs being met, the imperative of survival is progressively extinguished before the demand for comfort. Demand shifts to durable consumer products, which become the new engines of growth. In the 1930s, in Europe and the United States, the automobile and home appliances are symbols of this displacement. The salary, if initially remains a cost at the microeconomic level of the company, also reveals an income in the macroeconomic scale of the nation; it determines the drainage of the productive apparatus; there is a certain solidarity between incomes; it is by distributing wages that the companies, as a whole, support their sales, and it is by investing that they can distribute; as the bottleneck of capital has been broken, underemployment becomes essentially conjunctural, and it is with the resumption of growth that it becomes possible to re-establish employment. Going against the neoclassicists of that time, Henry Ford and John Maynard Keynes understand this, make spending a virtue, and advocate a policy of purchasing power, essentially conjunctural because, as Keynes says, 'in the long run, we will all be dead.'

(…)

At the end of this period, as the needs for durable consumer goods are saturated, they lose their driving role in development; a third phase is outlined, dominated by the satisfaction of the needs no longer affected by having, but by being. The immaterial, as we have seen, becomes the motor of a new mode of development symbolized by the computer. The relative evolution of the immaterial expenses (specially of the 'leisure-culture-health', to which we add today the whole set of services) allowed a prediction, already in the 50s, of the advent of the moment 'when this mutation […] without a doubt the most important of all those that have occurred up to the present day [...]would shift the economic leadership of material productions aimed at meeting saturable needs for activities whose material aspect is secondary and that meet unlimited needs.'

In the end, Passet (pp. 191) recognizes the ineffectiveness of the liberal State and says:

"Exclusion leads to revolt a youth without a future who can no longer bear the constant provocation of advertising that invites and incites to enjoy articles of consumption of which many are estranged for lack of training, employment, and income."

The historical analysis of the march and counter-march of the State requires us to understand that what changes the destinies of peoples is not their government in a subjective sense, but what objectively and effectively accomplishes for the material and immaterial development of the *homos politicus*, to whom the democratic State promises social justice.

Passet, in his analysis of commutative and distributive justice, inquires: *Is it not true that each person has the destiny he or she deserves? George Gilder, one of the American gurus of the school of offer, does not hesitate to diagnose: "The poor know... that they have chosen their situation, and can only blame themselves for where they are now." In what planet do those people live? (ob. cit. 112)*

The criminal's ethic, regardless of whether he is a white-collar criminal or not, is the same. His desire is to accumulate wealth to enjoy the maximum of assets that life can offer him, with the minimum commitment to justice, morality, or law. There is no concern for the "minimal welfare" or fear for the abusive inequalities that our formal democracies have created under the direct tutelage of legal positivism devoid of humanity.

The circumstances created by liberalism have potentiated the unethical conduct of the corrupt politician and the common criminal, who with the help of legal positivism have become aware of the opportunity and are well aware of using the means available for the fulfillment of their personal interests.

Politics was subjugated by the political class, which, in turn, subjugated economic science and law. With so much power, it has corrupted the social educational process and can thus gradually migrate from the act of corruption to the system of corruption as a real group of people for whom the crime pays off.

In this context, it is worth the infiltration of accomplices in penitentiaries, aiming at the elimination of witnesses of white-collar crimes and other acts of improbity with public money; it is also worth using people who "lend" their names to hide the source or recipient of illicit money to laundry the dirty money that came with the corrupt act, and, finally, the placing of representatives in the Branches of the government, as a form of self-preservation.

Forget about the stereotype of the drug dealer or the white-collar, lonely criminals who have no friends and stay home with closed curtains in a shady environment. This only happens in movies.

The modern criminal understood that the act of isolated corruption is solitary, yet the system of corruption allows him to live in social circles of friendship and parallel worlds in which he can run freely among his peers.

Norman Angell (2002 p.147), in addressing the shadowy interests of the political classes, says:

"It is as true today as it was at the time when Washington first said it, and as it will be forever, that we should expect no consequence from nations other than interest. This is, under the name of realism, the reason that declares German politics. From this, we can infer that the study of interests - international interests - is for the statesman the only basis of sound, sensible, and foreseeable action.

(…)

The old predatory instinct that induces the strong to seize by force of what they want remains (...) and by itself the moral energy is not enough to produce definitive results, except with the aid of material force. Governments are institutions, and institutions have no soul (...) They should first consult the interests of those who represent (...) their peoples. The instinct of supremacy forces countries to seek markets and, as far as possible, to exercise control over them by themselves and by force, definitive expression is possession (...) an inevitable link in a logical sequence chain: industry, markets, control, maritime bases."

In the scenario described above, politics subjugates the law and the economic science in order to create the perfect environment for industrialists, traders, financiers, and other class representatives to rise to power and pretend mercy and interest in the interests of the people. However, we have already asked, "On what planet do these subjugated people live in?"

Just as the people legitimize this system of corruption, only the people can make it come to an end. But how will it happen if the people have eyes, but they don't see and have ears, but they don't hear?

It is true that the perfect State is a fiction, but in history there is undeniable evidence of the power of the people, when it embraces its role as the active agent of history. It is at this moment that the democracy of empty promises is trapped by the duty to substantiate the minimum of social dignity, the only justification for accepting the State to govern over our lives.

# CHAPTER 2

# Further Thoughts on the Three Conceptions about the Influence of Law, Economics, and Politics in Government

Of all the sciences that contribute to organizing life in society, what most helps to finance, promote, and perpetuate corruption is politics.

Aristotle in *Nicomachean Ethics*, in the third century BC, already defended the supremacy of politics over the other sciences, although it must be remembered that politics according to his understanding was the ultimate end of ethical and moral man, different from the utilitarian politics that the ruling classes installed in the government of the States, as we know it today.

Here is an excerpt from Aristotle's thought on the influence of politics on the other sciences (1984: 49-50):

> "But the action of the statesman is also unleisurely, and – apart from the political action itself – aims at despotic powers and honors, or at all events happiness, for him and his fellow citizens – a happiness different from political action, and evidently sought as being different."

Now politics shows itself to be of this nature, for it is it which determines which sciences are to be studied in a State, which are to be learned by every citizen, and to what extent; and we see that even the most valued faculties, such as strategy, economics, and rhetoric, are subject to it. Now, since politics uses the other sciences and, on the other hand, legislates what we ought to do and what we ought not to do, the purpose of that science must encompass those of others, so that this purpose will be the human well being. Indeed, even if such an end is the same for both the individual and the State, the latter seems to be something larger and more complete, both to attain and to preserve. While it is well worth reaching for an individual, it is more beautiful and more divine to reach it for a nation or for city-states. These are, therefore, the ends intended by our investigation, since this belongs to political science as one of the meanings of the term.

Rene Passet (2002, pp. 222), when addressing the supremacy of politics and democracy over the economic science, says that *we all see the same reality, but we do not see it in the same way and we do not ask the same questions about it.* In one of his works, the author asserts (see p.235-236):

"2. The 'plural' economy

The collective interest also exists, irreducible to the former. The collective need does not come from the individual need; it is, as we have seen, of a different nature. The collective good does not fulfill any of the conditions of the formation of a price in the market. From the demand point of view, its service is both indivisible and simultaneously consumable by each one, without nothing being withdrawn from others: the sailor who is guided by the light of the lighthouse uses this light solely (it does not change attitude due to a price), still leaving it entirely available to others; unlike what happens with the individual good, which can only belong to one or another person, there is no competition for the possession of the collective good, and nothing obliges the consumer to reveal his preferences by offering a price, since no competition can deprive him of it. From the supply point of view, the collective good has no marginal cost: the construction of a piece of lighthouse is meaningless. It must be built entirely or it will be of no use; François Perroux called this type of investment 'bets on new structures'. In the absence of disclosure of preferences and marginal cost, the collective good is not part of the mercantile logic.

Its profitability is not revealed at the level of its exploitation account, but in that of the companies that surround it, and in the long run. The true economic efficacy of railways, for example, is not measured by their profits or losses, but by their contribution to the growth of the national product. It is even the deficit that can be rational here measured - and in the limit - in that it stimulates the creation of wealth that is superior to it.

What can one day finally about health or education? Let us consider them for a moment as mere intermediary goods valued in the light of commercial profitability. Evaluating them exclusively from a cost point of view, the dominant thought has hastened to declare the public institutions that are responsible for them as not profitable. Would the formation of spirits and the quality of health of men be meaningless? Let us consider literally the gentlemen of the Medef with the famous parable of Saint-Simon (1810): what would happen to the effectiveness of their companies, apparently the only creators of wealth, if tomorrow those monuments of supposed non-productivity, such as the educational system, the health system, the public transportation, and communications infrastructure system, all public services, would cease to exist?"

Professor Joseph LaPalombara (1982: 18-19), when comparing politics and governments says:

"It would be fantastic if I could say that political science, or even the whole group of social sciences, would be able to provide scientific guidance for the Perfect Society. Nevertheless, it is known that the main concern of the social sciences is man and the fulfillment of his noblest instincts and capacities (...)

More than two thousand years ago, Aristotle and his disciples studied the constitutions of 158 city-states, hoping to find the way to form the ideal *polis*. As we can witness from what we learn from any newspaper, more or less twenty centuries of experience, we cannot say that we are on the right track. (...)

This certainty comes from the certainty that the social sciences, including political science, are today, more than in the past, capable of understanding, explaining, and perhaps predicting the behavior of men and organizations."

In the fight for supremacy in the government of the democratic State, which holds law, economics, and politics, jurists think that power is in the law, while economists as important as Marx and Engels argue that it is the economy that conditions the government.

As we see it, law and economy are "pawns" on the board of the game of power, for, except for rare historical exceptions, politics has always sought to subjugate the State to the personal interests of those who are ruling at that moment.

Having studied the three conceptions that deal with the influence of law, economy, and politics in the State government, we restate the schematization we have constructed and introduced in Book 1, in order to justify our position on the supremacy of the political sphere in relation to the other sciences or arts that govern the State.

## 1 - LEGAL CONCEPTION
(defended by the actors of the law)

### LEGAL SPHERE
(believes that the safest direction of a state resides
in the hands of those who understand laws)

### POLITICAL SPHERE
(in theory, makes the laws according to the "spirit" of
cosmic justice -jusnaturalism, or according to the law of
good human reason-phenomenal positivism of Comte)

### OTHER SCIENCES
(are important for the government of the state and receive attention to the extent that they demonstrate greater utility for the governing legal class)

Under the mantle of logic and dialectics, economists reanalyzed the juridical conception, and when they realized that the domain of wealth was determinant for those who commanded and those who obeyed, they re-read the domain of the sciences and enthroned the economy over the others. This conception can be schematized by the following formula:

## 2 - ECONOMIC CONCEPTION
(defended by Karl Marx and Friedrich Engels, German philosophers
and economists, creators of the communist ideology)

### ECONOMIC SPHERE
(the phenomena that move life are the economic relations and, above
all, the control of the means of production of a community)

### POLITICAL SPHERE
(is the field of human domain in which the agent will or
will not realize the fair distribution of wealth by balancing
the means of production and the needs of the citizen)

## OTHER SCIENCES OR ARTS
(can represent a threat to the state if they are not ideologically useful)

Personally, I do not differ from the concept of politics as the science or art of government. It is the one that who creates, with the help of law, the rules that shape the character of the nation.

We understand that its dominion is absolute over other sciences and that political will is the most determining element of social acts and facts.

History is rich with examples of preponderance of the political domain over all other sciences.

Only war power has been able to resist despotic political power, but those who know either left or right dictatorships know how harmful to freedom they are.

This is the conception we formulate about the political domain in relation to the other sciences or arts that contribute to the state government:

## 3 - OUR CONCEPTION ON POLITICAL DOMINATION

### POLITICAL SPHERE
(power focuses on regimes of exception or is expressed in legislative, judicial, and executive functions in democracies co-opting accomplices useful for government activity)

### LEGAL SPHERE
(In formal democracies like those that currently prevail, the legal sphere is a mere useful tool for political actors. Their subproducts (such as laws) are more and more the means for purposes previously delimited by those in power or those who want to rule)

### OTHER SCIENCES
(they are important insofar as they concern the dominant political class and because of this they are subject to investment spikes when their products are ideologically useful)

Jesse Souza, Ph.D. in Sociology from the University of Heidelberg, Germany, (in the preface of *Democracy Today*) asks: - *What are the theoretical and practical consequences, from the increasing importance of the public sphere in various modern societies, of the relative loss of importance of the conception of the State as alpha and omega of political life?*

His quest objectively responds to positivize articulate modern social claims about economic equality, sexual orientation, race, and gender issues.

The problem that we see in the attempt to articulate these multiple factors lies in the fact that all social claims pass through the filter of politics as an art of government and, in the end, receive an ideological orientation of the "will" of the dominant classes, which, does not necessarily coincide with the "wanting" of the people.

Therefore, politics subjugates the right to positivize its authority and will by means of norms, and enslaves the other sciences to the purposes dictated by personal interests.

Politics causes statistics to disclose false data; directs science to the reproduction of non-innovative knowledge; conditions technology to the areas that most favor class dominance, and, ultimately, conditions the economy so that man becomes an object of consumption. It is no longer the man who is consuming objects, yet the objects that are consuming man.

Politics turns Economy into a market that produces disposable consumer goods. The model of the car is modernized every six months, the appliances become obsolete at the speed of sound, the electronic devices have to be renewed every four months or less and thus the *homos economicus* is directed to consumption in the political-legal system theater that subjects everyone in the name of the democratic State.

If politics preserved its Aristotelian conception of the ultimate goal of ethical and moral man, its dominance would be desirable. Nevertheless, it became an instrument of domination and oppression of the rich classes over the middle and the poor, withdrawing all their power from the public coffers, which they bleed on a regular basis.

I am fully aware that if this formal democracy and its political class are weighed in the balance of justice, it will be found at fault.

# CHAPTER 3

# Corruption as Enemy of Public Administrations

The State is a social institution whose area of activity is the public sector. The public sector, associated or not with the private sector, is responsible for the production and administration of goods and services destined to general well being.

From the political point of view, the State is the social institution with a form, system, and established government regime. When the State is led by the majority of the people, the regime is democratic. Otherwise, when directed by a ruler, it is a regime of exception.

The government of the State takes place though politics because politics is the science or art of governing

Brazil, for example, through its Federal Constitution of October 5th, 1988 elected to be a federative republic formed by the indissoluble union of states, municipalities, and federal district, being constituted into a democratic state. Therefore, decide on:

1 - the republican system of government;
2 - the representative system; and
3 - the democratic regime.

Needles to say that, without the seal of law, the form, the system, and the regime would not have support because it is the law that amalgamates the logic and the dialectic of the Social Contract, which structures the political or social man.

21

On the other hand, to say that it is democratic means that all power emanates from the people, who exercise it through elected or direct representatives. Some of the foundations of the State should be:

1 - sovereignty;
2 - citizenship;
3 - the dignity of the human being;
4 - the social values of labor and free enterprise;
5 - political pluralism.

In a State governed by the rule of law, social coexistence must reject any form of discrimination and promote, within natural inequality, as much equality as possible concerning social well-being.

It is impossible to understand the current context of democracy without attention to the humanist and developmental aspects of the most famous speech delivered by Lincoln, on November 19th, 1863, at the inauguration ceremony of the Gettysburg Military Cemetery, in which he reveals to dream for North America and the world to be:

> "...dedicated to the proposition that all men are created
> equal... government of the people, by the people, for the
> people, shall not perish from the earth..."

For political theory, the state is a social institution. Anna Maria Castro (1976:75) says that:

> "To understand an institution, it is necessary to know
> what it is made of. Being it a complex concept, formed
> of parts, it is necessary to know these parts, to explain
> each of them separately, and the way in which they are
> composed to form a set."

The modern state is made up of sovereign people, territory, and government. It is also seen as the manager of the public sector of the economy besides being the tutor of its own sovereignty.

Internally the engine that drives the State to achieve its democratic ends is its public administration, sometimes referred to the "administrative machine".

The public administration is composed of organs, entities, and public agents. It is incumbent upon it to provide efficient public services and administer the public treasury for the production of the general well being, also understood as the minimal happiness and well-being due to those who live in society.

Public administration can be thought according to objective and subjective criteria.

Objectively, it is defined by what it does for the citizen. Subjectively, it is the set of the organs, entities, and agents that compose it. In either case, its end is the general well being.

We can also say that objectively the public administration exists to provide services, intervene in the private economic domain when necessary, and foster national development through subsidies, financing, and partnerships with the private sector, among other activities that legally justify the production of general well being.

Subjectively, the public administration is the set of organs, entities, and public agents intended to make effective the objective criterion, that is, the provision of public services and social welfare that induces the "minimum of happiness" that is promised by the democratic state.

It is easy to perceive that both in an objective and subjective sense the public administration to be effective must yield to efficiency, as Diogo de Figueiredo Moreira Neto says (2008:14):

> "The States readjusted themselves, though not in a uniform way, as one would wish, by reason of cultural and level of development differences, in order to gradually overcome the beaten-up binomial - power-subjection - and replace it with the promising binomial - function-rights - in which the old ends of the State are re-read going from abstract idealizations, formulated by eventual ruling elites, or as old-fashioned truths contained in dusty ideological booklet, being now, simply, the realization of people's rights."

# 3.1 - The Enemies of the State and of the Public Administrations

The State exists and subsists while the people believe in its institutions. The legitimacy of State institutions, in turn, depends directly on the loyalty of the people to the foundations, principles, and objectives declared by the State. It also depends on the degree of maturity that the people have to discern whether the reward that is given is a formal or a substantial democracy in which their yearnings are more than promises stemming from unreal laws or impossible to be fulfilled.

Fustel de Coulanges (1975:265), based on the belief in Athenian democracy, said that the law punished malicious speakers and counselors:

"There was a law, little applicable indeed, that punished every orator convicted of having given the people bad advice. There was another that forbade access to the speaker's stand to any orator who had three times advised resolutions contrary to the existing laws."

In theory, we rely on democracy and the rule of legality as if this binomial were a guarantee of obedience by the subservient and loyalty of those who have the power. The people have proved loyalty to democracy and government, unlike rulers for whom the State is nothing but a great treasure worthy of being plundered. To succeed, they use captious principles such as hierarchy and legality that only work when the defendant is the common citizen.

Authority, obedience, and subordination are requirements of the theory of domination, a corollary of Political Theory, on which Anna Maria Castro and Edmundo F. Dias explain (1976: 137):

"One must understand by "domination", (...) the probability of finding obedience within a given group to specific assignments (or for all kinds of assignments). It does not, therefore, consist in any kind of probability of exercising "power" or "influence" over other men. In this case, this domination ("authority"), as indicated, can be seen on the most diverse reasons of submission: from the unconscious habit to what is purely rational considerations for certain purposes. A certain minimum degree of will to obey, or of interest (external or internal) in obeying, is essential to every authentic relationship of authority."

Jessé Torres Pereira Junior (1991:3) writes on the concept of domination in law, as follows:

"All power, regardless of its nature, is to be exercised as an instrument of distribution of justice and promotion of social peace. (...) So, the powers and duties of authority and the individual rights of those who must surrender to the public or collective interests find legal balance."

We believe it is possible to infer from Carmen Alcalde (1972:143), quoting the State Theory of Thomas Hobbes, an approach to the theory of domination when it speaks of value and morality. Here is the excerpt:

"En la elaboración de su teoría del Estado, Hobbes parte de la igualdad entre todos los hombres. La enemistad y el odio surgido entre ellos proviene de la insatisfacción de sus aspiraciones; recuérdese la antigua máxima latina: homo hominis lupus (el hombre es lobo para el hombre)."

Benedetto Croce (1988:7) surrendered to the principle of authority and in the quest for thinkers to write a bill of rights received from Mahatma Gandhi a letter with the following reflection:

"I learned from my illiterate but wise mother that all rights to be deserved and preserved came from duty well done. Thus, the very right to live accrues to us only when we do the duty of citizenship of the world. From this one fundamental statement, perhaps it is easy enough to define the duties of Man and Woman and correlate every right to some corresponding duty to be first performed. Every other right can be shown to be usurpation hardly worth fighting for."

Maria Stela Grossi Porto (2006:99) draws attention to the dilemma recognition versus social resentment, as a problem in which we must carefully work care because *a society that operates with maximum recognition and a minimum of resentment ensures its governability, as well as, on the contrary, maximum resentment and a minimum of recognition are a sure condemnation of disorder and decay.*

It is known that the State is voracious in its hunger to collect, but narrow in distribution of wealth and dignity. Being that if it is certain that the tax collection is always insufficient to provide the public needs, it is also certain that the resentment is increasing among the population that more and more realize how much corruption prevents the effectiveness of public policies given the subtle enemies.

Among the many enemies of public treasury, we cite the following:

1st - fortuitous cases;
2nd - waste;
3rd - indeterminate concepts;
4th - corruption.

# 3.1.1 - Fortuitous Cases or Natural Events

Fortuitous cases or natural events, such as floods, landslides, droughts, earthquakes, storms, tsunamis, and so on, cause damage to public treasury, even though they are, almost always, unforeseeable and inevitable.

When foreseeable and the resulting damage is due to the negligence of the government, conscious and free omission from the authorities must generate civil, criminal, and administrative liability. Sanctions may include the dismissal of public office or employment, destitution of a commission, or even loss of term, as stated in Articles 34 to 36 and 85 of the 1988 Brazilian Constitution and further laws.

Imagine that a local executive branch chief neglects the installation of lightning rods in a location where lightning strikes frequently and because of such electric discharges the home appliances of the taxpayers are damaged. Imagine, also, that the responsible public authority does not oversee the construction of a dam wall and it breaks flooding surrounding cities. In such cases, the negligence of the administrator must be civilly, criminally, and administratively liable.

Public administration probity is a commandment for any and all public agents with or without power. Since the public manager is aware and free from subjugation of illegality or perpetrated illegitimacy, such conducts must be sanctioned, so that impunity does not have an educational effect contrary to what ethics, morality, and law preach.

# 3.1.2 - Waste

Waste is one of the reflexes of inefficiency because efficient means the one who manages with speed, productivity and adequacy.

Nowadays when sustainability is becoming a doctrine, the waste of human and material resources by public managers needs to be sanctioned with the loss of the position, job, function, or term and with the consequent repair of the damages caused to treasury.

Unfinished public works, purchases and hiring of services without planning or with poor planning, irresponsible biddings, totally denying the principle of reasonableness, are examples of how the public administration wastes its material resources.

Waste has a brutal impact on human resources, as public contests and other forms of entry into the public service require more and more expertise from candidates, but when they receive their assignments, they realize that the best paid positions are for campaign staff, relatives, and friends for whom meritocracy does not apply.

Commissioned and expert advice positions are distributed among the various political groups that "bundle" in congresses. Those who rebel against the system are ideologically persecuted or have their career isolated because they constitute a threat to the corrupt ones who "bleed" the coffers of the nation and, therefore, to the possibility of implementing the public policies that the democratic state promises but does not fulfill.

When the aforementioned conducts are practiced in a free and conscious way to harm the public treasury and are left unpunished, the State neglects the force of law and weakens justice.

On the other hand, it strengthens in the population the feeling that the ethical, moral, and legal behavior charged by the State only applies to the poor and ordinary citizens, while for the rich and corrupt civil servants, crime pays off.

Broken public coffers are synonymous with fallacious public policies and a formal democracy that promises housing and leaves the citizens homeless, promises energy and relegates men to darkness, promises health, transportation, safety, and employment, and ultimately delivers crystallized speeches in the form of a law, instead of social dignity.

Waste drains the energy that the State accumulates with its human and material resources.

# 3.1.3 - The Danger of Indeterminate Concepts — Discretion

Indeterminate concepts are dangerous because of the discretion they leave to the political class and to malicious public managers.

It is typical of the politician to edit laws that will need further regulation. This happens because, when regulating higher laws by means of lower standards, this politician can later insert any kind of indetermination that favors interpreting the law in a personal way or in a way that benefits interested third parties.

We all know that a promise is a future and uncertain event. In politics, it is a rule to promise and to break what is promised.

When beginning a term knowing that it will not be able to fulfill the promises of campaign, the solution found by the legislators is to make laws in which rights are created, yet impossible to be implemented.

Politicians are masters in sophistry, in the use of difficult words as a way to confuse the brain of others and, thus, make their empty speech prevail. The formula succeeds all over the world.

Karl Otto Erdmann, a German philosopher and linguist (*in Arthur Schopenhauer, 38 Ways to Win An Argument* -Faro Publishers, pages 14-15), cites five examples of indeterminacy that help to conquer debates and which are traditionally used by who holds the power or by whom he wishes to rule him:

1 - language inadequacy from the logical point of view. Goethe states: "So one talks, the person already begins to wander;"
2 - conflict between the universal and the individual: the dangers of generalization, schematization, and typification; the contradictions and the imperfections of induction;
3 - the fact that our main convictions are based on values and, therefore, are linked to the idea of right and wrong;
4 - the inevitable phenomenon that each experience is given at the same time as that of others and that no one can reject the authorities;

5 - the eradicable tendency of all people to absolute thought, and how much our values, concepts, and knowledge are relative.

Note that the political class follows those five orientations almost literally in order to win the trust of its electorate. After taking office it feels disengaged with the people and committed to the interests of the group that elected it or the political group with which it is committed.

In his inner being, the corrupt man takes office, job, function or term thinking about benefiting or to benefit third parties. Reason why when making laws that create, modify, transform, or extinguish rights, the corrupt inserts indeterminate concepts so lawyers can spread doubts and, with the help of corrupt public officials, everyone can benefit from the coffers of the republic.

Cincunegui (1996:113) asserts that one of the causes that most favor corruption is discretion because of its indeterminate concepts. Here is how he presents it:

"Hemos señalado en diversos pasajes de este trabajo, que uno de las causas que da lugar a mayor corrupción es la discrecionalidad administrativa, entre la cual se encuentra la denominada "técnica" a la que hemos aludido precedentemente.

La doctrina de los conceptos jurídicos indeterminados originada en Alemania, supone una restricción a la discrecionalidad, permitiendo la intervención judicial frente a conceptos definidos en forma general en las leyes, tales como "oferta más conveniente", "idoneidad", "tarifas razonables y justas", "eficiencia empresaria", etc., los que hay que distinguir de conceptos de valor tales como "bienestar general", "interés público", "bien común", etc.

Con respecto a estos últimos, no existe facultad discrecional, y deben ser aplicados a las resoluciones mediante un análisis previo de los fundamentos, los medios y los fines o consecuencias, reflexionando y llevando a cabo juicios de valor de manera de conocer si lo que se resuelve en realidad se ajusta al bien jurídico que se trata de resguardar o fortalecer."

All that is indeterminate is waiting for something or someone to determine it.

The proliferation of indeterminate concepts in Law stimulates the manager to treat the public affairs according to his understanding and not according to what determines justice and moral. He, at most, will do what the law determines, knowing that on numerous occasions the law has already been made under the ideological bias of the group to which he owes an explanation.

Considering this hypothesis, the objectivity of the law is replaced by the subjectivity of the public agent and the social interest replaced by the many personal interests that determine the application of public monies.

# 3.1.4 - Corruption, a Seductive Enemy

Corruption has a special "charm." Those who corrupt themselves consciously and freely do so for subjective reasons, almost impossible to be known in their entirety. However, the conquest of wealth and power are the two greatest appeals it offers.

Luxurious property assets and differentiated *status quo* easily seduce anyone who is predisposed to corruption and are highly tempted, even those who are ethical.

The ability to resist is in the inner being because it is there that consciousness is persuaded or not. It is the soul-will, in the conscious and free man that will determine the commissive or omissive conduct, the result of which will entail the betrayal of the trust of the people who elected the individual to the position, job, function, or term.

We have seen these as enemies of the public coffers:

1st - fortuitous cases;

2nd - waste;

3rd - indeterminate concepts;

4th – corruption

Among those four enemies of the State, the most lethal is corruption. Being it active or passive, the fact is that it annually pays sufficient amounts to significantly minimize problems of health, housing, transportation, safety, leisure, labor, or education in any of Mercosur countries and the world.

If we are aware of this truth, why don't we want to solve the problem of corruption related to public resources? Who benefits from the chaos created by systemic corruption?

Corruption, if not fought, can spread in government, politics, and State administration. Mendieta (2000: 24) in dealing with the limits of public morality teaches:

"Pues bien, es en dicho entorno donde quisiera situarme ahora. En primer lugar es necesario saber qué límites no se deben franquear y, posteriormente, definir los valores que deben guiar la conducta dentro de la frontera ya segura de la moralidad pública. Dicho esto, la primera cuestión que se nos plantea cuando hablamos de corrupción en la acción de gobierno es la de los niveles de corrupción. No es lo mismo la corrupción del régimen político, la corrupción política y la corrupción administrativa. En ocasiones, el régimen político en su totalidad es corrupto. De acuerdo con Aristóteles, las formas legítimas de gobierno son definidas de acuerdo con su contribución al bien común: en la monarquía uno solo gobierna de acuerdo al bien común, en la aristocracia los mejores lo hacen, mientras que en la república la mayoría gobierna de acuerdo a lo común. Por el contrario, en las formas corruptas de gobierno (tiranía, oligarquía y democracia) se ejerce el poder para satisfacer intereses particulares (Del Águila, 1998, p. 29)."

The report of the *Oficina Anticorrupción, Ministerio de Justicia y Derechos Humanos de Argentina* (2004: 33), in response to the claims of prevention against corruption in *Convención de Naciones Unidas Contra la Corrupción* mentions:

"El ámbito de las contrataciones públicas es sin duda uno de los que mayor interés concita cuando de corrupción se habla. La principal interfase de relación entre el Estado y el sector privado lo constituyen las adquisiciones públicas. Las contrataciones públicas suponen gastos en miles de millones anualmente y representan indudablemente seductoras oportunidades para aquellos que buscan ventajas ilegítimas."

On the duty to give public transparency to public biddings and the control system, the above report (2004: 35-36) repeats the following UN recommendations:

"1. Cada Estado Parte, de conformidad con los principios fundamentales de su ordenamiento jurídico, adoptará las medidas necesarias para establecer sistemas apropiados de contratación pública, basados en la transparencia, la competencia y criterios objetivos de adopción de decisiones, que sean eficaces, entre otras cosas, para prevenir la corrupción. Esos sistemas, en cuya aplicación se podrán tener en cuenta valores mínimos apropiados, deberán abordar, entreoirás cosas:

a) La difusión pública de información relativa a procedimientos de contratación pública y contratos, incluida información sobre licitaciones e información pertinente u oportuna sobre la adjudicación de contratos, a fin de que los licitadores potenciales dispongan de tiempo suficiente para preparar y presentar sus ofertas;

b) La formulación previa de las condiciones de participación, incluidos criterios de selección y adjudicación y reglas de licitación, así como su publicación;

c) La aplicación de criterios objetivos y predeterminados para la adopción de decisiones sobre contratación pública a fin de facilitar la ulterior verificación de la aplicación correcta de las reglas o procedimientos;

d) Un mecanismo eficaz de examen interno, incluido un sistema eficaz de apelación, para garantizar recursos y soluciones legales en el caso de que no se respeten las reglas o los procedimientos establecidos conforme al presente párrafo;

e) Cuando proceda, la adopción de medidas para reglamentar las cuestiones relativas al personal encargado de la contratación pública, en particular declaraciones de interés respecto de determinadas contrataciones públicas, procedimientos de preselección y requisitos de capacitación.

2. Cada Estado Parte, de conformidad con ¡os principios fundamentales de su ordenamiento jurídico, adoptará medidas apropiadas para promover la transparencia y la obligación de rendir cuentas en la gestión de la hacienda pública. Esas medidas abarcarán, entre otras cosas:

a) Procedimientos para la aprobación del presupuesto nacional;

b) La presentación oportuna de información sobre gastos e ingresos;

c) Un sistema de normas de contabilidad y auditoría, así como la supervisión correspondiente;

d) Sistemas eficaces y eficientes de gestión de riesgos y control interno; y

e) Cuando proceda, ¡a adopción de medidas correctivas en caso de incumplimiento de los requisitos establecidos en el presente párrafo.

3. Cada Estado Parte, de conformidad con los principios fundamentales de su derecho interno, adoptará las medidas que sean necesarias en los ámbitos civil y administrativo para preservar la integridad de los libros y registros contables, estados financieros u otros documentos relacionados con los gastos e ingresos públicos y para prevenir la falsificación de esos documentos.

A fin de concentrar nuestro análisis en los aspectos principales del texto, comentaremos en profundidad sólo el punto 1 de la prescripción que se refiere, justamente, al problema de las contrataciones dejando para otra oportunidad un estudio más detallado sobre el punto 2.

El primer elemento a destacar es la obligatoriedad de estas disposiciones que se denota a partir del uso de los verbos 'adoptará' en la primera parte del encabezado y el 'deberán abordar' referido a las medidas en particular al final del acápite.

Los principios establecidos por el artículo son, a nuestro criterio, sumamente apropiados; se sostienen la transparencia, la competencia y los criterios objetivos de adopción de decisiones como base para procesos de compra eficientes. El concepto de criterios objetivos es a la vez novedoso y útil. La exigencia de guías imparciales aplicables a las distintas etapas de la contratación es uno de los mejores instrumentos para prevenir situaciones de corrupción, ya que la posibilidad de los oferentes de conocer con anticipación los criterios que se utilizarán para definir la adjudicación de los contratos públicos es fundamental como elemento de certeza en el proceso, que permite entonces evitar gran parte de las situaciones de corrupción relacionadas con decisiones arbitrarias y además establece las condiciones para una gestión pública eficiente, fijando parámetros que hacen mucho más sencilla la tarea del funcionario público encargado de recomendar la adjudicación y de aquel que, en definitiva, debe tomar la decisión sobre la asignación del contrato."

In short, public transparency depends on measures such as:

1 - wide publicity of administrative acts;
2 - bidding with objective criteria and effective control;
3 - an effective appeal system:
4 - criteria for training of personnel; and
5 - control of public accounts accountability.

José Ariel Núñes (2006:37) says that there are three enemies of Public Administration. Among them, he also highlights corruption. So he states:

"Los tres enemigos de La Administracción Pública:

• La evasión fiscal
• El despilfarro: hacienda del Rey y hacienda del pueblo
• La corrupción"

Professor José Armando da Costa (2000:12) also identifies the lethal power of corruption over probity and notes:

"Will today's reality be any different? From here onwards, have the principles of decency and probity been reintroduced and revived in the various quarters of public affairs, including the legislative, executive, and judicial branches in the three spheres of government of our federal State, as our honored and blessed ancestors intended? According to the data that daily fill the material conveyed by our media, the answer is very negative and worrying."

# 3.2 - Corruption and Impunity

From our younger days, our parents try to correct our deviations from conduct. The argument has always been and will be to teach ethical conscience in order to instill in each child respect for his neighbor, as well as for his material and non-material goods.

This educational process is revealed to us by all the social groups with which we live or of which we are part, that the rights and duties are reciprocal, reason why the State is in charge of protecting the most varied assets, such as life, property, honor, physical or mental integrity, individual freedom and, also, probity in the public administration, among others.

The State, due to its growing influence, became the guardian of social assets and, because of the services rendered to the community and the added danger in such activities, was forced to considerably expand its legal protection.

For example, because of the need to protect the circulation of its currency, the State typified crimes against public faith; to protect our privacy, it has criminalized infringement of domicile and breach of correspondence.

In the field of the responsibilities of the public agents, we migrate from the absolutist understanding of "the king can do no wrong" to the subjective guilt and later to the objective guilt of the State, in which guilt or malice cease to be important in the face of prejudice caused to third parties by public agents.

We live under a social pact in which we have been indoctrinated to believe in the infallibility of the State. A kind of political theology has been created in the collective consciousness in which the State and its laws are confused with God and his commandments. Whoever disobeys is punished.

The question is: Is anyone who disobeys really punished, or does it depend on who disobeys?

The law is this commandment emanating from "divine" goodness, which subjugates everyone. The problem is when we realize that although we all have a corrupt nature, not everyone who allows himself to be corrupted is treated equally by the law. An example of this is when the law grants immunities and privileged forum to political agents.

This legal protection of the political agents and the benefits that make them different from the regular citizens transforms the act of corruption into a system of corruption in which the corrupt ones protect themselves using the own government system.

The corrupt from the executive branch protects the corrupt from the legislative branch that protects the corrupt from judicial branch. In this vicious and corporate cycle, only the people are left without protection.

Impunity is like fire in dry field. In the educational process, impunity creates men with ethics and legal consciousness different from what universal justice requires.

For these men "genetically" modified by corruption, subjugating is the rule, sharing is the exception, and honesty is a relative concept

Scholars agree on the common belief that impunity is one of the most effective causes of corruption.

Juan S. Pegoraro (1999:6) when writing about corruption as a social and criminal matter says:

> "Actualmente la característica más relevante de la corrupción es la impunidad, porque el problema si bien parece pertenecer a la incapacidad del sistema legal-penal, excede ese ámbito y pasa a las instituciones en conjunto: la conducta corrupta es algo así como la punta de un iceberg y sus partes sumergidas son las instituciones del estado, en especial el sistema penal. Los funcionarios públicos, sean electos o nombrados por otros de mayor jerarquía en la administración pública, actúan en la realidad como miembros pertenecientes a una 'corporación' o un 'estamento' y se saben investidos de un fuero especial como es la impunidad. La corrupción como conducta no sería sólo explicada por la utilidad económica que representa para el actor sino que hay que incluir esa conducta en la

> red de relaciones sociales entretejidas con la vida política
> y con el arte de gobernar, la dinámica social de la lucha
> por el poder y los vínculos y conflictos sociales y políticos.
> En este entretejido se incluye la impunidad."

Pegoraro also affirms that the most relevant characteristic of corruption is impunity. José Ricardo Etkin (1993:266) also refers to the ills of impunity:

> "Al igual que en la perversidad, lo patológico de la
> corrupción es la impunidad y la existencia de factores
> estructurales en las propias organizaciones que llevan a la
> instalación y mantenimiento de estas injusticias. En este
> sentido las denuncias y sanciones aisladas no permiten
> disimular que el problema está en el funcionamiento de
> las instituciones."

Democracy was born as a movement and crystallized as a monument because it solidified as a regime of promises, it became a formal democracy, when everyone expected it to be substantial, to fulfill what it says, to give the people housing, transportation, health, safety, education in quantity and quality; that makes man evolve from freedom to equality and, ultimately, to fraternity.

We corroborate with Professor of the University of Pisa, Antonio A. Martino, when he says:

> "There is no democracy of thieves, but there are thieves
> who, if tolerated, sooner or later will ruin democracy."

Impunity is the worst example that can be given to society, since society's character ends up suffering the influence of impunity, absorbing its meaning as the logic of living.

In the wake of this understanding, impunity becomes not only the current language, but also the dominant one, that is, it becomes the ideology expressed by some and secreted by others.

At this stage, the idea of educating the new generations with another thought becomes an illusion, given that impunity becomes a customary model of the "paths and layers" of the conscious and collective unconscious.

# 3.3 - Corruption and Illicit Enrichment

Corruption involving public money is destined to illicitly enrich politicians, public officials, and third parties that act as a group with delinquent purposes.

In his book *El Derecho Penal: doctrina y jurisprudencia*, Guillermo Ariel Todarello (2005:6) when comparing the Argentine Penal Law with the phenomenon of corruption and illicit enrichment says:

> "En tal sentido cabe destacar que la corrupción ha sido entendida básicamente como la apropiación privada, en forma ilegal, de un bien público."

Mariano Grondona (1993:20) also sees corruption as a source of illicit enrichment:

> "Los actos de corrupción pueden ser clasificados según su gravedad. El primer grado es el de la propina o regalo que se ofrece como signo de gentileza o gratitud. El segundo grado es la exacción, esto es, la extorsión de un funcionario a un ciudadano para que pague por obtener lo que, de todos modos, le es debido. Por último, existe el cohecho, pago que se ofrece para que un funcionario haga lo que no es debido."

In Europe, the Professor of the *Universidad Complutense de Madrid*, Manuel Villoria Mendieta (2000:84), addressing the excessive and superfluous spending of public money states:

> "El enriquecimiento inapropiado de los miembros del gobierno o altos cargos de la nación es otro tema incorporado normalmente a los escándalos. Por dicha razón dimitió recientemente el ministro británico Mandelson, debido a la ocultación de un préstamo facilitado por un correligionario, o se acaba de producir la dimisión del presidente de Israel, también por otro préstamo dudoso. La ausencia de plena honradez fiscal llevó a la dimisión

al ministro español de Agricultura, Vicente Albero, o ha
estado presente en las múltiples peticiones de dimisión del
ex portavoz del Gobierno y luego ministro de Relaciones
Exteriores, Josep Piqué."

The cases of misappropriation of public funds become a systemic
learning process for the new generations of corrupts who are now part of
the body of the public administration.

Emile Durkheim, in dealing with the sociological process of education,
teaches that:

> "education has precisely the purpose of forming the
> social; one can then perceive, as if in a summary, how this
> being was constituted through history. Constant pressure
> that the child suffers from the social environment trying
> to mold it into its image, pressure that both parents and
> teachers are only the representatives and intermediaries."
> (Introduction to Sociological Thought – Eldorado – 4th
> edition – p. 84)

Now, if corruption is learned, the way to fight it must also be learned.
Virgolini (2004:37) says:

> "Estas perspectivas estaban contenidas en los trabajos
> del propio SUTHERLAND sobre la asociación diferencial
> y la organización social diferencia – formuladas por
> primera vez en sus Principies of Criminology, en 1939,
> y desarrolladas más tarde en la edición de 1947–, al
> señalar la existencia de una organización diferenciada
> con objetivos criminales, dentro de la cual la conducta
> criminal es el resultado de un proceso de aprendizaje que
> no difiere sustancialmente de cualquier otro aprendizaje
> orientado a la conformidad.
>     Para SUTHERLAND, el proceso se compone de los
> siguientes puntos: a) el comportamiento criminal es un
> comportamiento aprendido; b) tal comportamiento se
> aprende a través del contacto con otras personas y por
> medio de procesos de comunicación; c) es aprendido en

el marco de relaciones interpersonales directas; d) junto con el comportamiento criminal se aprenden también las técnicas necesarias para la comisión del delito y una orientación específica que se vincula con los motivos, las tendencias impulsivas, las valoraciones y las actitudes en relación con el crimen: e) la orientación impresa a los motivos y a las tendencias impulsivas dependen de la interpretación, favorable o desfavorable, de los principios sancionados por las leyes; f) se deviene criminal cuando las interpretaciones contrarias al respeto a la ley son prevalecientes respecto de aquéllas favorables; g) las asociaciones diferenciales pueden variar en relación a la / frecuencia, duración, prioridad e intensidad del contagio; h) el proceso de aprendizaje del comportamiento criminal implica los mismos mecanismos empleados en cualquier otro tipo de aprendizaje; i) aunque el comportamiento criminal es la expresión de un complejo de necesidades y de valores, no se puede explicar en estos términos como criterio diferencial, dado que también el comportamiento honesto tiene como referencia las mismas necesidades y valores."

Sutherland, quoted by Virgolini, in his *Princípios de Criminologia* lists nine behaviors on the learning process of corruption. We highlight the following:

1) criminal behavior is learned;
2) such behavior is learned through contact with other corrupts and through the communication process;
3) the process is learned within the framework of interpersonal relationships;
4) along with criminal behavior, one learns the necessary techniques necessary to commit crimes;
5) the corrupt reads between the lines of the law, always aiming personal benefits;
6) the group of people committing crimes or acts of corruption occur according to the frequency, duration, priority, and intensity of the results that will be produced;

7) The process of criminal learning is similar to any cognitive process.

Doctor Rupert Prizl (2000:138-139), in turn, believes that the public official over time realizes that it is not their productive activity that generates wealth, but corruption. So, he begins to foster himself and others with it. Here is how he clearly exposes his understanding:

"Con el tiempo y la experiencia, las partes involucradas en los ilícitos comprenden que no son las actividades productivas las que proveen los mayores ingresos adicionales, sino las prácticas corruptas. Por eso canalizan sus esfuerzos en pos de crear y preservar sus fuentes de ingresos ilegales (más actividad política, politización del funcionariado, etc.). De este modo se generan efectos dinámicos de aprendizaje.

Existen situaciones en que los funcionarios públicos reciben una escasa remuneración regular y se ven prácticamente impulsados a complementar sus ingresos por medio de actividades ilegales. En tales circunstancias, cualquier compromiso profesional serio en cuanto a tiempo y energía puede conducir a que la función pública sea obstructora o incluso contraproducente para tener acceso a ingresos ilegales y aprovechar los mismos. Un juicio similar emite el Banco Mundial:

'El acceso a ingresos adicionales puede convertirse en la actividad principal obligada. Los empleados públicos no harán nada sin soborno de por medio, y una gran parte de la población estará ocupada en tareas improductivas, destinadas a ganar su favor o comprar su silencio. La corrupción puede convertirse así en la verdadera justificación de la existencia de instituciones, en lugar de ser apenas un aspecto insignificante de su actividad.'(...)

'The real problem is not that there are no honest bureaucrats, but rather that there are sufficiently many dishonest men who are held together by the bond of self-interest and who act together as a block when opposed by any single honest person'."

Pritzl points out in the last paragraph that the main problem in relation to the corruption process is not the inexistence of honest bureaucrats, but the fact that there are many dishonest people who join together as a group of people and crimes to defend their own interests, as opposed to any honest person. This corrupt system ends up by co-opting accomplices and by threatening employees who do not wish to adhere to dominant practices.

We believe that if the State does not develop effective means to fight corruption, it will devour it as a cancer that, once in the body, will become metastasized.

The effective formula is to make and enforce national and international anti-corruption laws, such as the Inter-American Convention Against Corruption (IACAC), among others we address in this book.

At the end of this work, it will be proved that the Mercosur states have effective laws and that the lack of a solution to date is the lack of political will to use law as a tool to fight corruption, as Manuel Hespanha (2005:455) points out:

> "The idea of an alternative use of law is, to some extent, more outdated than the proposals of a critical criticism of critical schools. It is based on the idea that the use of law is not hopelessly repressive and favorable to the dominant groups, and it is possible to carry out, from within the law itself and with legal instruments, progressive and liberating tasks. For this, however, certain conditions, some methodological, some institutional, would be necessary."

# CHAPTER 4

# The Political and Legal Importance of Creating and Strengthening Anti-Corruption Structures

This chapter begins by repeating the wise words of José Ariel Nuñez, who affirmed the importance of educating the spirit of man in the fight against corruption since laws, organizations, and instrumental techniques are tools of men and women conditioned by the environment in which they live. Nuñez states (2006: 21-22, 23):

> "El control público es un producto de segregación social. No es un valor aislado. El deviene de una relación con los demás valores sociales imperantes en la sociedad, tales como la política, la economía, el Derecho, y muy especialmente los principios morales y la Justicia. (…) Porque las leyes, las organizaciones y las técnicas serán finalmente instrumentales de hombres y mujeres condicionados por el medio social."

We add to Nuñez's understanding the creation and strengthening of anti-corruption institutions according to Rodolfo Luis Vigo (2006: 301):

> "...la renuncia a las instituciones sociales traería para Alexy aparejada la anarquía, ello en base a los tres problemas apunta dos en el terreno del conocimiento, de la ejecución y de la organización."

The creation and strengthening of anti-corruption institutions is one of the main concerns of supranational political bodies, like the UN, which recommends through Article 36 of the UNCAC - United Nations Convention Against Corruption that:

> "Cada Estado Parte, de conformidad con los principios fundamentales de su ordenamiento jurídico, se cerciorará de que dispone de uno o más órganos o personas especializadas en la lucha contra la corrupción mediante la aplicación coercitiva de la ley. Ese órgano u órganos o esas personas gozarán de la independencia necesaria, conforme a los principios fundamentales del ordenamiento jurídico del Estado Parte, para que puedan desempeñar sus funciones con eficacia y sin presiones indebidas. Deberá proporcionarse a esas personas o al personal de ese órgano u órganos formación adecuada y recursos suficientes para el desempeño de sus funciones."

Note that the UNCAC recommends that each participant State ensure that it has one or more bodies as well as specialized personnel in the fight against corruption.

Manuel Villoria Mendieta (2000: 154,157-158), in his work *Ética Pública y Corrupción,* makes it clear that without the support of political leaders and a vigilant society, any attempt to control corruption is ineffective:

> "Dichos líderes deben lanzar claros mensajes de que no admitirán la corrupción. El apoyo a sistemas de financiación transparentes de los partidos políticos es uno de los instrumentos esenciales para emitir un mensaje de apoyo a la moralidad en la vida pública. Además, ha de procurarse que la actuación de todos y cada uno de los responsables de unidades administrativas sea coherente con estos mensajes y, para ello, debe sancionarse cualquier desviación de la conducta ética ejecutada por tales directivos, tan pronto como se produzca (…)
>
> Ya sea a través de los medios de comunicación, ya a través de las asociaciones ciudadanas, la sociedad civil debe estar alerta y denunciar cualquier conducta incorrecta.

El asociacionismo es el principal elemento constitutivo de la sociedad civil y su manifestación más visible. Por ello, de su fuerza, de su capacidad para estar presentes en el debate y en la resolución de problemas, dependerá que una sociedad cuente con espacios públicos suficientemente sólidos como para asumir responsabilidades, vigilar y controlar la actuación de los poderes públicos y garantizar la autonomía de lo civil (pero público) frente a la política (que no agota ese espacio público) (Subirats, 1999, page 6).

The structures or institutions of control need to act efficiently and effectively within the internal and the external scope.

Mendieta (2000: 170-171) says that judicial control *"Es el más importante método de control externo,"* and also states that:

"Esto implica que, dado que la Administración tiene que actuar «de modo racional y razonable» (T. R. Fernández, 1994, p. 199), el Tribunal que juzgue su actuación puede:

a) Controlar si la Administración ha tomado en consideración los elementos que debe tener en cuenta o si, por el contrario, ha omitido alguno —test de racionalidad.

b) Si, aun habiendo tomado en cuenta esos elementos, ha llegado o no a una conclusión razonable —test de razonabilidad.

c) Excepcionalmente, se puede llegar a sustituir una decisión administrativa por otra decidida por el juez. En Estados Unidos, por ejemplo, el juez puede elegir la solución más razonable de las posibles. En España no se llega tan lejos, y el juez tan sólo adopta la única decisión que, en el curso del proceso, ha quedado en pie. Es decir, si, existiendo dos posibles decisiones, la adoptada por la Administración es considerada ilícita, el juez puede imponer la lícita, sea o no políticamente pertinente."

We believe it is important to remember that Mercosur member countries are signatories to the CICC and that this was the first convention to fight corruption, serving as a paradigm for the UNCAC.

In this study of comparative law carried out in Mercosur member countries, we have observed the existence of several public institutions focused on supervising accounting, financial, budgetary, operational, and assets of the organs and entities of the public administrations of those countries, which proves, as Hector Mairal (2007: 94-95) said, that the norm by norm mentality is not enough to make the law effective. Here is how he points this out:

> "Recordemos la conocida frase de LORD ACTON: "Absolute power corrupts absolutely." Las tradicionales reglas del Estado de Derecho no solo defienden la libertad de los ciudadanos sino también sirven para combatir la corrupción. Pero no basta con la vigencia teórica de esas reglas. Es necesario que ellas sean observadas en la práctica y no desnaturalizadas por normas de rango menor. (…) Ya lo había previsto ALBERDI cuando advirtió que "es preciso que el derecho administrativo no sea un medio falaz de eliminar o escamotear las libertades y garantías constitucionales."(…)
>
> En este trabajo hemos identificado una de dichas condiciones básicas: La indefensión del ciudadano frente al poder del Estado. "La corrupción acompaña al poder como la sombra al cuerpo" ha dicho bien ALEJANDRO NIETO. Por ello, pretender eliminar o reducir la corrupción sin limitar el poder que, como representantes del Estado, ejercen hoy día los funcionarios públicos argentinos, es ilusorio."

Law alone has no power to prevent or reduce corruption to bearable limits. In fact, law is often manipulated and made an ally of corruption, either through prodigality to create indeterminate concepts, or to confer excess of discretion, even when it is excessively bureaucratic. After all, it is useful to create difficulty in selling facilities to the corrupt.

Law, the greatest input of the democratic state, is not enough to break with the culture of corruption, especially when it focuses on the powers of the republic, for as Lord Acton said, *absolute power corrupts absolutely.*

# 4.1 - The Government in the Sunshine Act

Have you noticed that when a ray of sunlight enters a dark room, its straight path becomes visible because of dust particles hanging in the air?

Have you ever wondered why the corrupt acts secretly? Why does he camouflage his actions?

The answer is that no offender likes to expose himself in the light of law or justice, even when the sanctions provided are favorable to them. Behold, one way or another, what affects most is not to be weighed in the scales of law, but to stop the flow of easy gain by embezzling public funds.

This is the philosophy embedded in the North American Transparency Act called Government in the Sunshine. It aspires to reveal the "filthy act" that the corrupt try to hide.

Cincunegui (1996: 65-66, 67) makes the following digression about the mentioned law:

> "La ley de transparencia denominada "Government in the sunshine" fue dictada en 1976, habiendo entrado en vigencia en 1977. Su nombre deriva de una declaración del Juez Brandéis quien manifestó que "la publicidad es justamente un remedio para la enfermedad social e industrial. La luz del sol ("sunlight") es el mejor desinfectante, y la luz eléctrica el más eficiente policía".
>
> La ley requiere que la mayoría de las reuniones de los miembros de las agencias gubernamentales se efectúen en público, prohibiendo las comunicaciones secretas por el personal de las agencias durante procedimientos adjudicatorios (adjudicatory) o de fijación de reglas (rule-making). (...)
>
> Por otra parte, estas normas no son otra cosa que el reconocimiento a las tendencias que la transformación mundial - especialmente de la mano de la revolución informática y su incidencia en las comunicaciones—, provocará en la vida y desarrollo de los países con sistemas de gobierno democráticos."

What is regrettable regarding the systems of control is that they have the purpose of exposing corruption to the law when they should expose it to the "sun of justice." Behold, justice always wants law, but law does not always want justice.

Of course, since the control system is a threat, the corrupt will do everything possible to have control over the control system.

One of the factors that allows the subversion of control lies in the power to draft laws that ensure nominations under the seal of the heads of any of the powers of the State. The result is that one pretends to control and the other pretends to let himself be controlled. In the end, they all make a fortune out of the public coffers, while the people are impoverished and the country stumbles along the path of development.

# 4.2 - Institutions of State Control in Mercosur

The Mercosur countries adopted the French theory of separation and harmony of powers.

We did research trips *in loco* and in each one of the members of Mercosur we observed the existence of norms of internal and external control of all the branches of the government.

It is a common rule in the member countries that the Legislative Branch externally controls the budgetary, financial, accounting, assets, and operational aspects of the Executive and Judicial branches.

The Judiciary, in turn, exercises control of the legality and legitimacy of judicial and administrative acts.

The law also enables the Executive Branch, in addition to the internal control of its administrative acts, the political control that the President may exercise by vetoing laws approved by the Legislative Branch.

Thus, the independent political powers are harmonized in the task of governing the *res publicae* and controlling of one over the other.

What one has to realize is that fighting corruption requires much more than the isolated action of the branches of any of the Mercosur countries since corruption has become part of their culture. Either the people get involved in the system of control or the actions of the State will always be evasive in publicizing the quantity and quality of the institutions that control the resources of the Nation.

# 4.2.1 — In Argentina

In Argentina, the 1999/2000 Management Report (2002: 45-46) of the Department of Justice demonstrates that corruption control tools exist and are known, as can be inferred from the following excerpt:

> "Emprender políticas activas contra la corrupción estatal constituyó una de las premisas fundamentales del nuevo gobierno. La ley de ministerios (n° 25.233) creó en el ámbito del Ministerio de Justicia y Derechos Humanos, un órgano nuevo en el cuadro institucional argentino: la Oficina Anticorrupción, cuyas funciones sustanciales son la investigación preliminar de aquellos hechos que pudieran constituir delitos reprimidos por la Convención Interamericana contra la Corrupción, denunciarlos penalmente y hacerse parte querellante en los casos más relevantes, evaluar y controlar las declaraciones juradas de los funcionarios en cuanto a su eventual enriquecimiento ilícito o incompatibilidad en el ejercicio de la función, y elaborar programas de transparencia y de prevención de la corrupción." (2000: 49)

The Argentine Constitution of 1994 also provides for other bodies within the sphere of the Legislative Power, such as: the National Audit Office (Article 85) and the Ombudsman's Office (Article 86). However, a commission to monitor compliance with the Inter-American Convention Against Corruption, composed by the bar of lawyers in the federal capital concluded there was an overlapping of the organs and excessive and inefficient legislative oversight.

Too much control can actually lead to no control. It is up to the people to identify subtle strategies of the political class that overlap organ over entity and entity over entity, precisely to mask the lack of quality, as well as the number of individuals and legal entities supposedly destined to that end.

Here is an excerpt from the aforementioned Argentina report, which addresses the issue of quantity and quality of control:

"a) Del análisis de las funciones y misiones de los Organismos Públicos requeridos se advierte que en muchos casos las tareas que le fueran encomendadas se superponen, siendo ejercidas por varios Organismos simultáneamente.

Esta dispersión y superposición genera un innecesario desgaste de recursos de Estado, lo que no resulta una política conveniente ni efectiva en las actuales condiciones en que se desenvuelve el país.

b) En aquellos aspectos que hacen a los controles internos existe un exceso normativo (por ejemplo, duplicidad de Códigos de Ética Pública dentro del mismo Poder Ejecutivo Nacional); y en otros aspectos, tales como el establecimiento de sanciones para quienes violen las disposiciones obligatorias, hay una orfandad que conspira contra el sistema que la Convención establece.

c) En lo que respecta a la publicidad y contenido de las declaraciones juradas patrimoniales y financieras de los funcionarios públicos, se encontró —y verificó— que en los diferentes poderes del Estado no hay uniformidad de criterio para su cumplimiento..."

As it has been shown, there are competent rules and institutions, but there is a lack of political-juridical will to implement an effective fight against corruption at the national and international levels within Mercosur.

Having rules and institutions to fight corruption and not using them is like being a person who has both legs, but who does not want to walk.

Guillermo Ariel Todarello, in dealing with the system of control of corruption, says that it lacks independence to the individuals and legal entities entrusted with such a task.

It also says that management controls are carried out irregularly, that there is a system of protection for witnesses and whistleblowers, that there is a lack of cross-control to detect acts and systems of corruption, and that accountability is flawed.

Todarello says (2008: 159-160):

"— Con relación a este punto se denuncia la falta de independencia que caracteriza a los sistemas de control, como así también su connivencia con el poder político, ello como una de las razones más relevantes en punto a la ineficacia de su tarea. Dicha falta de independencia se pone de manifiesto, por ejemplo, cuando el poder ejecutivo designa los auditores que deben controlar a los ministros nombrados por ese mismo poder.

— Los controles de gestión se ejercen de manera irregular. No se evalúan los costos de los programas ni su eficacia, sino el aspecto formal, basado en el cumplimiento mecánico de la normativa (reglamentación, contabilidad, chequeos de firmas).

— Ausencia de un adecuado sistema de protección de testigos y denunciantes. Las amenazas de despido han conspirado para que los empleados que hayan presenciado irregularidades decidan no denunciarlas.

— Se destaca la existencia de normativa destinada a limitar la intervención de la auditoría en ciertas áreas, tales como los organismos descentralizados, o los privados que mantienen convenios de cooperación con instituciones públicas y de financiamiento internacional.

— Se advierte acerca de la conformación de una "administración pública paralela", la cual resulta financiada mediante recursos de organismos internacionales, y cuyo gasto y ejecución del presupuesto se encuentra sometido a un sistema de control alternativo o diferente al empleado por la administración pública.

— Ausencia de controles cruzados, circunstancia que evidentemente garantizaría niveles más adecuados de transparencia.

— También se verifica la ausencia de control y de rendición de cuentas respecto de aquellos organismos, asociaciones, empresas v fundaciones a los que se transfieren fondos, quienes a su vez se amparan en aquella normativa que exime a estos organismos de los procesos de auditoría intenta y externa."

# 4.2.1.1 - Todarello vs. Mairal: Views on Control and Public Transparency in Argentina

By comparing the understanding of both authors on the subject, one can see how much they coincide in their strategies to fight against corruption. What needs to be done is just to assess the tools to fight the phenomenon. Here is how they present the subject:

| Guillermo Ariel Todarello (preventive strategies) | Hector Mairal |
|---|---|
| 1 — education | 1 — previous control |
| 2 — civic and moral education | 2 — citizen participation or popular control |
| 3 — raise awareness | 3 — transparency on public decisions |
| | 4 – deep judicial control |

The preventive strategies cited by Todarello (2008: 212) are very clear and part of common sense. In order to leave no doubt about what the civic and moral education mention, here is the explanation:

> "a) Como instrucción, la educación se relaciona básicamente con reglas técnicas, las cuales señalan qué medios deben ser utilizados para alcanzar un objetivo específico. La transmisión de conocimientos científico-técnicos o la enseñanza de oficios pueden constituir ejemplos de este tipo de educación.
>
> b) La educación cívica, por otra parte, consiste en la enseñanza de valores morales. A través de ella se transmiten determinados principios que son tomados como referencia para realizar acciones. Por medio de la educación cívica se adquieren hábitos, se modifican comportamientos y, en definitiva, se logran estilos de vida."

The strategies adopted by Héctor Mairal, such as prior control, popular participation, transparency of public decisions, and deep judicial control, have been known since the middle of the last century. Note that in many reforms on public control the idea is nothing more than old news.

In Brazil, the control rules are provided for in the Public Accounting Code of 1922, replaced by Decree-Law Number 200/1967 and subsequently maintained by the 1988 Constitution, especially Articles 70 and 71 thereof. There are numerous rules on control.

Therefore, Mairal complains when he says (2007: 66):

> "La misma proliferación de los controles conspira contra su eficacia: '**En este país de los miles de controles, en realidad no existe ningún control verdadero porque existen demasiados.**' La observación sobre la realidad italiana es también pertinente para nuestro país." (bold print by the author)

In a country with innumerous systems of control, there is actually no control at all simply because there too many to count. The didactic wrath of Mairal is absolutely sound.

We believe that preventive and repressive strategies can be effective if the people are educated to fight and if there is between them and the agents who deal with public money a sort of pact of integrity, as exemplified by Todarello (2008: 266-269):

> "El pacto de integridad es un instrumento desarrollado por la organización no gubernamental Transparencia Internacional con el objetivo de que los gobiernos y los miembros de la sociedad civil que estén dispuestos a luchar contra la corrupción puedan utilizarlo en el ámbito de la adjudicación de contratos públicos. Dicho mecanismo ayuda a reforzar la confianza de la población respecto del procedimiento de adjudicación por parte de las autoridades, y contribuye a acrecentar la credibilidad en el proceder de gobiernos y administraciones.
>
> En concreto, consiste en promover un acuerdo entre las diferentes partes contratantes, en virtud del cual tales se comprometen a desarrollar su actuación de manera

> transparente, aceptando, asimismo, la intervención de un
> organismo de control y el sometimiento a las sanciones
> previstas en caso de incumplimiento de la palabra
> otorgada."

# 4.2.2 – In Brazil

What has been said for Argentina can be repeated *ipsis litteris* for all members of the Mercosur. First, because the legal system is the same (Roman-German law with few autochthonous input), and second because the political system is identical (republican form, representative system, and democratic regime).

In Brazil, the Constitution establishes that the internal control is done by each branch of the Government and the federal external control by Congress with the help of the Federal Court of Accounts. This is the formula provided for in Articles 70 and 71 of the Constitution of the Federal Republic of Brazil of 1988.

"Article 70. Control of accounts, finances, budget, operations and property of the Union and of the agencies of the direct and indirect administration, as to lawfulness, legitimacy, economic efficiency, application of subsidies and waiver of revenues, shall be exercised by the National Congress, by means of external control and of the internal control system of each branch (CA No. 19, 1998)

Sole paragraph. Accounts shall be rendered by any individual or corporation, public or private, which uses, collects, keeps, manages, or administers public monies, assets or values, or those for which the Union is responsible or which, on behalf of the Union, assumes obligations of a pecuniary nature.

Article 71. External control, incumbent on the National Congress, shall be exercised with the aid of the Federal Court of Account, which shall:

I.    examine the accounts rendered annually by the President of the Republic, by means of a prior opinion which shall be prepared in sixty days counted from receipt;

II.   evaluate the accounts of the administrators and other persons responsible for public monies, assets, and values of the direct and indirect administration, including foundations and companies instituted and maintained by the Federal Government as well as the accounts of those who have caused a loss, misplacement or other irregularity resulting in losses to the public treasury;

III. examine, for the purpose of registration, the lawfulness of acts of admission of personnel, on any account, in the direct and indirect administration, including the foundations instituted and maintained by the Federal Government, with the exception of the appointments to commission offices, as well as the granting of civil and military retirement and pensions, except for subsequent improvements which do not alter the legal fundaments of the conceding act;

IV. carry out, on its own initiative or on that of the House of Representatives, of the Senate, or of a technical or inquiry committee, inspection and audits of an accounting, financial, budgetary, operational or property nature in the administrative units of the Legislative, Executive and Judicial Powers and other entities referred to in item II;

V. control the national accounts of supranational companies in whose capital stock the Union holds a direct or indirect interest, as set forth in the acts of incorporation;

VI. control the use of any funds transferred by the Union, by means of an agreement, arrangement, adjustment or any other similar instrument, to a state, the Federal District or a municipality;

VII. render the information requested by the Congress, by either of its Houses or by any of the respective committees concerning accounting, financial, budgetary, operational and property control and the results of audits and inspections made;

VIII. in case of illegal expenses or irregular accounts, apply to the responsible parties the sanctions provided by law, which shall establish, among other combinations, a fine proportional to the damages caused to the public treasury;

IX. determine a period of time for the agency or entity to take the necessary steps for the strict compliance with the law, if an illegality is established;

X. if not heeded, stop the execution of the impugned act, notifying the House of Representatives and the Senate of such decision;

XI.    present a formal charge to the competent Branch on any irregularities or abuses verified.

Paragraph 1. In the case of a contract, the restraining act shall be adopted directly by the National Congress, which shall immediately request the Executive Power to take the applicable measures.

Paragraph 2. If the National Congress or the Executive Power, within ninety days, do not take the measures provided for in the preceding paragraph, the Court shall decide on the matter.

Paragraph 3. Decisions of the Court resulting in the imposition of a debt or fine shall have the effectiveness of an execution instrument.

Paragraph 4. The Court shall, quarterly and annually, forward to the National Congress a report on its activities.

In the scope of the Federal Executive Branch, in addition to the control performed by internal audits, there are the following institutions that can be used to control corruption:

1)    The Comptroller General of the Union – CGU
2)    Federal Attorney General - AGU
3)    Public Defender of the Union – DPU

Article 127 to 129 of the Brazilian Federal Constitution of 1988 gives exceptional powers to the Public Prosecution Service to exercise control. We can highlight:

"Article 129. The following are institutional functions of the Public Prosecution Service:

I.     to initiate, exclusively, public criminal prosecution, under the terms of the law;
II.    to ensure effective respect by the Public Authorities and by the services of public relevance for the rights guaranteed in this Constitution, taking the action required to guarantee such rights;
III.   to institute civil investigation and public civil suit to protect public and social property, the environment and other diffuse and collective interests;
IV.    to institute action of unconstitutionality or representation for purposes of intervention by the Union or by the states, in the cases established in this Constitution;

V.  to defend judicially the rights and interests of the Indian populations;

VI.  to issue notifications in administrative procedures within its competence, requesting information and documents to support them, under the terms of the respective supplementary law;

VII.  to exercise external control over police activities, under the terms of the supplementary law mentioned in the previous article;

VIII.  to request investigatory procedures and the institution of police investigation, indicating the legal grounds of its procedural acts;

IX.  to exercise other functions which may be conferred upon it, provided that they are compatible with its purpose, being forbidden judicial representation and judicial consultation for public entities."

The judicial branch, which follows the North American system of checks and balances, is still the most respected control body known in the democratic system.

However, when we read on the news about judges selling judgment decision, selling *habeas corpus,* and top court justices selling or swapping their opinions and votes for money or personal favors, the general feeling towards the branch declines and the fear that the democratic state is rotten in its foundations leads us to think that its institutions need reconstruction.

The legislative branch (Article 70 of the Brazilian Constitution) assisted by the Federal Court of Accounts (corresponding to the Contraloria General de La Nación, in the other Mercosur countries), controls the other branches of the government externally, as it has already been demonstrated.

Other politico-legal control bodies, such as the Financial Activities Control Council (COAF), continue to be created in the hope that the system will work. The COAF established that (1999: 13):

> "In March 1998, Brazil, following on from commitments made since the signing of the Vienna Convention of 1988, approved Law No. 9,613, which represents a step forward in addressing the issue, as it typifies the crime of money laundering. It also establishes measures that give greater responsibility to economic and financial intermediaries and creates, within the scope

of the Department of Finance, the Financial Activities Control Council (COAF)."

Brazil has committed itself internationally to the political-legal fight against corruption. Here are some historical milestones of the international agreements on money laundering mentioned in the book *State Advocacy: Institutional Issues for Building a State of Justice: Studies in Homage to Diogo de Figueiredo Moreira Neto* (2009: 472-473):

"1. United Nations Convention against Illicit Traffic in Narcotic Drugs and Psychotropic Substances, 1988, Vienna;

2. The 40 recommendations on money laundering of the 1990 Financial Action Task Force (GAFI/FATF), revised in 1996 and referred to as GAFI/FATF Recommendations;

3. Elaboration by the Inter-American Drug Abuse Control Commission (CICAD) and approval by the General Assembly of the Organization of American States (OAS) of the 1992 Model Regulations Concerning Laundering Offenses Relating to Illicit Drug Trafficking and Other Crimes;

4. The Ministerial Communiqué of the Summit of the Americas Conference Concerning the Laundering of Proceeds and Instrumentalities of Crime, 1995, Buenos Aires; (BRAZIL/UN Financial Control Council. Money Laundering: a world problem. Brasília: UNDC P, 1999. Page 21.)"

Jefferson Cárus Guedes and Luciane Moessa Souza state:
"It is precisely for the purpose of guaranteeing the application of the principles of legality and legitimacy that the legal advice performed by the Federal Attorney General's Office is characterized as a real control function in the political process (in the light of Karl Loewenstein's functional classification). By ensuring that public policies formulated within the executive branch are in accordance with the legal system, both at the constitutional and legal levels, legal advice makes it possible for the public administrator to be held accountable for his acts, since he cannot rely

on a supposed efficiency in meeting the social demands to stop obeying the law and the Constitution.

Drawing on Bruce Ackerman's equally innovative classification of State functions, one can consider the role of the Federal Attorney General as a veritable integrity branch designed to fight corruption and similar abuses in favor of probity in the public sphere.

It is incumbent upon the Attorney General of the Union, in its advisory role to defend the public interest of the State, analyzing the feasibility or infeasibility of public policies, based on the legal system. In addition, in order to be able to exercise its function of controlling legality and legitimacy, control institutions need to promote constant articulation with other organs and entities, not only public, but also private.

It is necessary to understand the exact repercussion of a given public policy that is being formulated so that legal advice to the executive branch is not made only on the basis of an abstract reading of the law and the Constitution. It is not for another reason that in Loewenstein's thinking the control function cannot be viewed in isolation from the mechanisms of political leadership, which are clearly revealed in the work of the executive branch."

# 4.2.3 – In Uruguay

About the State control system in Uruguay, the *Asociacion de Magistrados del Uruguay* promoted in April, 1988, in Montevideo, the seminar about *El poder judicial frente a la corrupción* (1998: 38-39, 52-54) and from his Annals we draw the following conclusion:

> "III) QUE HACE EL ESTADO FRENTE A LA CORRUPCIÓN Finalmente, el último control lo tiene el cuerpo electoral. Ha de ser el más importante y no hay otro tan legítimo como éste. Si bien está latente de continuo a lo largo de cada período de gobierno, se manifiesta muy espaciadamente en el tiempo y cuando lo hace desaprobando una función, los daños de la corrupción pueden ser de mucha proporción e irreparables. — (...)
> Posibilidades de una lucha eficaz contra la corrupción

En particular cabe mencionar las siguientes medidas destinadas a combatir la corrupción:

- Gestar una alianza entre fuerzas políticas, sociedad, administración pública, sector privado, justicia y ciudadanía con el propósito de impedir una mayor propagación de la corrupción y combatir eficazmente la ya existente. Evitar aspectos vulnerables en los trámites administrativos, lograr una mayor seguridad en cada uno de los pasos administrativos y ejercer un control sobre los mismos.

- Implementar medidas de prevención contra la corrupción analizadas en función de objetivos fijados según los aspectos específicos del sistema y relacionados también con aspectos inherentes a la naturaleza humana, siendo siempre el eslabón más débil el hombre.

- Implementar una reforma administrativa que permita una mayor transparencia en el desarrollo de las tentativas y decisiones.

- Analizar en forma sistemática la estructura de los organismos oficiales con el propósito de detectar situaciones que abren la puerta a la corrupción. Una posible medida es acelerar el despacho de los trámites, simplificarlos y adoptar medidas tendientes a su desburocratización y a la inserción de adecuados mecanismos de control.

- Flexibilizar la política presupuestaria a fin de mejorar el control sobre el manejo del gasto y la posible corrupción que pueda emanar de tal situación.

- Replantear la política de privatización de empresas públicas y de la llamada "tercerización" de servicios para someterla a un régimen de control más severo.

- Fiscalización de cada uno de los diferentes pasos en la elaboración de planes en la administración pública y estricto cumplimiento de las reglas que regulan las licitaciones públicas.

- Estricto control de proyectos y adjudicación de contratos al igual que la evaluación de las ofertas a los efectos de verificar si han sido formuladas correctamente, se compadecen con el criterio de rentabilidad y son comparables en cuanto a los precios ofertados.

- Aunque no siempre sea posible hacerlo, es importante evitar trabajar en forma apresurada, en condiciones de escaso tiempo disponible, porque ello deriva con frecuencia en una situación en la que se cumplen las reglas vigentes para el llamado a licitaciones y los procedimientos de elaboración de proyecto y adjudicación.

- Evitar una superposición de competencias o la posibilidad de que un funcionario se exceda en sus funciones, al igual que el llamado "nepotismo".
- Contratar auditores internos que fiscalicen a intervalos regulares las prácticas administrativas y cuya labor sea complementada por la convocatoria de auditores externos.
- Ejercer un mayor control vertical y horizontal.
- Sensibilizar en forma personal a los servidores públicos para los problemas que crea la corrupción.
- Excluir la posibilidad de que un funcionario pueda reunir en su persona diferentes cargos públicos que muchas veces representan intereses encontrados.
- Desarrollar sistemas de indicadores que permitan un control puntual de distintos funcionarios, al fin de detectar más fácilmente a las prácticas de corrupción.

Existen además múltiples medidas preventivas que pueden adoptarse en forma complementaria. Sin embargo, el éxito de tales medidas dependerá siempre de las condiciones prevalecientes en cada país. (…)

Corrupción y control: el rol del Tribunal de Cuentas en el ámbito internacional

La segunda parte de esta exposición estará dedicada a hacer una breve reseña de la actuación del Tribunal de Cuentas de Uruguay en el ámbito internacional en el tema que hoy nos ocupa.

Las Entidades Fiscalizadoras Superiores (Tribunales de Cuentas, Contralorías, Contralores, Cortes de Cuentas, cualquiera sea el nombre y la organización que tengan en cada país) están nucleadas en un organismo internacional llamado INTOSAI, en el cual el Tribunal de Cuentas de Uruguay ha tenido una activa y destaca actuación los últimos años y particularmente en el tema que estamos tratando. La INTOSAI es la organización profesional de Entidades Fiscalizadoras Superiores (EFS) de los países pertenecientes a las Naciones Unidas. Fue fundada en

1953, hace ya más de cuarenta años por las EFS de treinta y cuatro países, y en la actualidad cuenta con ciento setenta y seis miembros. Esta organización proporciona el marco institucional para el intercambio de experiencias y el enriquecimiento mutuo de las EFS, a los efectos de que las mismas sean capaces de enfrentar las demandas y expectativas que las sociedades les plantean. Porque hoy en día en todo el mundo se reconoce la importancia de la auditoría gubernamental. Y este avance va acompañado de una conciencia cada vez mayor acerca del significativo papel que desempeñan las EFS en cada país, multiplicando las demandas y expectativas respecto a las mismas. La INTOSAI apoya a sus miembros a avanzar para un mejor cumplimiento de estas expectativas, proporcionándoles la oportunidad de compartir información y experiencias respecto a los retos que el mundo de hoy, cambiante y cada vez más interdependiente plantea con respecto a la fiscalización y valoración. En su carácter de organismo pionero internacionalmente reconocido dentro de la fiscalización del sector público, la INTOSAI da a conocer pautas internacionales para la gestión financiera y también para otras áreas, desarrolla metodologías afines, proporciona formación y promueve el intercambio de información entre sus miembros. Trabaja en cinco idiomas: español, alemán, árabe, francés e inglés y lleva a cabo su misión y cumple con sus objetivos a través de diversos órganos, a saber:

- El Congreso Internacional de Entidades Fiscalizadoras Superiores (INTOSAI). Este Congreso se realiza cada tres años, teniendo como anfitrión uno de los países miembros. De este modo INTOSAI brinda a todos sus miembros la oportunidad de reunirse para debatir los temas de interés conjunto, compartir experiencias y aprobar pautas comunes de actuación. Los últimos tres congresos se realizaron en Berlín, Washington y El Cairo, y el próximo tendrá lugar en nuestro país en noviembre de este año. A partir de su realización, el Tribunal de Cuentas de Uruguay pasará a presidir dicho Organismo internacional por tres años (hasta el próximo

Congreso), y luego seguirá integrando el Comité Directivo por seis años más. En la actualidad Uruguay ya es el Primer Vicepresidente de INTOSAI.

- El Comité Directivo, que cuenta con diecisiete miembros (Egipto (Presidente), Uruguay (Primer Vicepresidente), Arabia Saudita (Segundo Vicepresidente), Estados Unidos, Australia, Austria, Barbados, Brasil, Camerún, Canadá, Alemania, India, México, Marruecos, Noruega, Portugal y Tonga) y se reúne anualmente. Es el órgano de Dirección que da continuidad a la actuación de la Organización durante los tres años que median entre uno y otro Congreso. Su presidencia corresponde a la EFS del país anfitrión del último Congreso. Con el objeto de garantizar una representación equilibrada de todos los países miembros, en el Comité están representados los siete Grupos de Trabajo Regionales y los principales tipos de sistemas de fiscalización del sector público.

La Secretaría General, que constituye el soporte administrativo central de INTOSAI, está situada en Viena (Austria) y el Secretario General es el Presidente del Tribunal de Cuentas de Austria. Gestiona el presupuesto de la Organización, está al servicio del Comité y de los Congresos, facilita las comunicaciones entre los miembros y organiza seminarios, estudios especiales y publicaciones.

Los Grupos de Trabajo Regionales. Existen siete grupos de trabajo que promueven los objetivos de INTOSAI en el ámbito regional, y brindan a sus miembros la oportunidad de centrar su atención en cuestiones específicas que interesan a cada región. Estos grupos de trabajo son:

OLACE FS — Organización de EFS de América Latina y del Caribe
AFROSAI — Organización de EFS de África
ARA BOSAI — Organización Árabe de EFS
ASOSAI — Organización de las EFS de Asia
SPASAI — Organización de EFS del Pacífico Sur
CAROSAI — Organización de EFS del Caribe

EUROSAI — Organización de EFS de Europa."

From the proceedings of the Seminar in Montevideo one can, in summary, extract the following recommendations for the fight against corruption:

1 - forge an alliance between political forces, society, public administration, and the private sector in order to prevent the spread of corruption;
2 - implement measures to prevent corruption;
3 - implement administrative reforms that allow greater transparency in decisions;
4 - systematically analyze the structure of official bodies to detect situations that open doors to corruption;
5 - adjust the budgetary policy to improve the management of the expenses and its control;
6 - redesign the privatization policy;
7 - intensely monitor of bidding procedures;
8 - avoid superimposition of competences;
9 - avoid nepotism;
10 - privilege internal audit and exercise greater vertical and horizontal control, among other measures, that can also be taken.

# 4.2.4 – In Paraguay

The Paraguayan control system is the same as the other systems of Mercosur member countries. The country has the internal control within the scope of each branch, and the external control is done by organs like the Comptroller General. Of the researches that we carried out *in loco*, we can emphasize the following laws and control organs:

"— Ley n° 1.626, de la función pública — Ley n° 2880/2006, que reprime hechos punibles contra el patrimonio del estado;
— Ley 2.051/2002, de contrataciones públicas, que establece el sistema de contrataciones del sector público

y tiene por objeto regular las acciones de planeamiento, programación, presupuesto, contratación, ejecución, erogación y control de las adquisiciones y locaciones de todo tipo de bienes, la contratación de servicios en general, los de consultoría y de las obras públicas y los servicios relacionados con las mismas;

— Ley n° 2523, que previene, tipifica y sanciona el enriquecimiento ilícito en la función publica y el tráfico de influencias;

— Ley n° 2777/2005, que prohíbe el nepotismo en la función pública.

— Ley n° 1.160, código penal."

From our research trips to Mercosur member countries, we became aware of the various budgetary, financial, patrimonial, and operational control organs of the State. In Paraguay, Evelio Fernández Arévalos (2003: 457-461) asserts:

"En otros casos la Constitución Nacional adopta la forma abierta, que establece algunas atribuciones, deberes, competencias y modos de funcionamiento explícitos del órgano, pero delega expresamente en la ley la facilidad o el mandato de ampliarlas, utilizando generalmente la fórmula "los demás deberes y atribuciones que fije esta Constitución y la ley" (delegación constitucional a la ley).

Son algunos casos de forma abierta y de delegación constitucional a ley:

—la Procuraduría General de la República (Art. 246 C.N.);

—el Consejo de la Magistratura (Art. 264 C.N.);

—el Ministerio Público (Art. 268);

—la Contraloría General de la República (Art. 283 C.N.), y

—la Defensoría del Pueblo (Art. 279 C.N.).

La Contraloría General de la República es, pues, un órgano constitucional extra-poderes del estado, de forma abierta, ya que respecto de sus atribuciones, deberes y competencias, el Art. 283, inciso 8) C.N., efectúa una expresa delegación constitucional a la ley.

De esta manera, dada su forma abierta, los deberes y atribuciones especificados en el Art. 283 C.N., pueden ser ampliados y modalizados en virtud de esa delegación constitucional a la ley, aunque siempre respetando las características definitorias y las funciones de la institución, delimitados en los Arts. 281, 282, 283 y 284, C.N.

c) La función central de la Contraloría General de la República es de control de las actividades económicas y financieras de los órganos públicos, lo cual excluye su actividad preventiva o ex ante así como el ejercicio potestades ejecutivas, legisferantes o directivas: no puede dirigir a los órganos sujetos a su control ni imponerles deberes."

Article 249 of the Paraguayan Constitution gave the Comptroller General power to exercise control over all other branches of the government. The text is as follows:

"Artículo 249 — DE LA AUTARQUÍA PRESUPUESTARIA

El Poder Judicial goza de autonomía presupuestaria. En el Presupuesto General de la Nación se le asignará una cantidad no inferior al tres por ciento del presupuesto de la Administración Central.

El presupuesto del Poder Judicial será aprobado por el congreso, y la Contraloría General de la República verificará todos sus gastos e inversiones."

Dentre os órgãos de controle merece citação especial, por seu papel constitucional, a Contraloría General de la República, conforme transcrevemos abaixo:

"La Contraloría General de la República es el órgano de control de las actividades económicas y financieras del Estado, de los departamentos y de las municipalidades, en la forma determinada por esta Constitución y por la ley. Gozará de autonomía funcional y administrativa.

(...)

El Presidente de la República, en su carácter de titular de la administración del Estado, enviará a la Contraloría la liquidación del presupuesto del año anterior, dentro de los cuatro meses del siguiente. En los cuatro meses posteriores, la Contraloría deberá elevar informe y dictamen al Congreso, para que los consideren cada una de las Cámaras.

(...)

Son deberes y atribuciones del Contralor General de la República:

el control, la vigilancia y la fiscalización de los bienes públicos y del patrimonio del Estado, los de las entidades regionales o departamentales, los de las municipalidades, los del Banco Central y los de los demás bancos del Estado o mixtos, los de las entidades autónomas, autárquicas o descentralizadas, así como los de las empresas del Estado o mixtas;

el control de la ejecución y de la liquidación del Presupuesto General de la Nación;

el control de la ejecución y de la liquidación de los presupuestos de todas las reparticiones mencionadas en el inciso 1, como asimismo el examen de sus cuentas, fondos e inventarios;

la fiscalización de las cuentas nacionales de las empresas o entidades multinacionales, de cuyo capital participe el Estado en forma directa o indirecta, en los términos de los respectivos tratados;

el requerimiento de informes sobre la gestión fiscal y patrimonial a toda persona o entidad pública, mixta o privada que administre fondos, servicios públicos o bienes del Estado, a las entidades regionales o departamentales y a los municipios, todas las cuales deben poner a su disposición la documentación y los comprobantes requeridos para el mejor cumplimiento de sus funciones;

la recepción de las declaraciones juradas de bienes de los funcionarios públicos, así como la formación de un registro de las mismas y la producción de dictámenes sobre la correspondencia entre tales declaraciones, prestadas al asumir los respectivos cargos, y las que los aludidos funcionarios formulen al cesar en ellos.

la denuncia a la justicia ordinaria y al Poder Ejecutivo de todo delito siendo solidariamente responsable, por omisión o desviación, con los órganos sometidos a su control, cuando éstos actuasen con deficiencia o negligencia, y

los demás deberes y atribuciones que fije esta Constitución y las leyes."

The comparative study that we have done on the legislation of Mercosur member countries leaves no doubt as to the existence of full symmetry of the rules of budgetary, financial, accounting, patrimonial, and operational control, as well as the control of legality and legitimacy of political and administrative acts.

Our observation of the existence of symmetry in the rules of control within Mercosur countries allows us to say that the lack of combativeness to corruption that bleeds the public coffers stems from a lack of political and judicial will and not from the absence of laws or legitimate institutions.

# 4.2.5 – In Venezuela

As in the other member countries of Mercosur, legislative symmetry is a legal reality in Venezuela. There is the system of internal and external control operationalized by constitutional and infra-constitutional institutions.

A reading on the competences *Contraloria General de la República*, in *Resolución Número 01-00-00-0145 30,* from April, 1997, clearly supports what we have been mentioning. Here are some excerpts from the norm:

> "CONTRALORÍA GENERAL DE LA REPÚBLICA
> República de Venezuela
> - Contraloría General de la República, Despacho del Contralor General de la República. Caracas, 30 de Abril de 1997.
> - Resolución Número 01-00-000145 186° y 138°
> El Contralor General de la República, de conformidad con lo dispuesto en los artículos 54, 69, 70 y 72 de la Ley Orgánica de la Contraloría General de la República y en ejercicio de la atribución que le confiere el numeral 4 del artículo 15 del Reglamento Interno de este Organismo Contralor.
>
> CONSIDERANDO:
> Que a la Contraloría General de la República, como órgano rector de los sistemas de control interno y externo de la Administración Pública Nacional, le compete dictar las normas e instrucciones para el funcionamiento coordinado de dichos sistemas, y que es fundamental para tal funcionamiento la prescripción uniforme de los mismos;
>
> CONSIDERANDO:
> Que para ejercer un control ágil y eficaz, se requiere que las entidades y organismos públicos establezcan y mantengan adecuados controles internos, de forma tal

que el control fiscal externo se complemente con el que le corresponde ejercer a la administración activa;

CONSIDERANDO:
Que la existencia de normas reguladoras del control Interno de las entidades y organismos faculta el ejercido de las potestades de orientación, coordinación, ordenación y evaluación que sobre el mismo tiene igualmente asignadas la Contraloría General de la República; resuelve dictar las siguientes:

NORMAS GENERALES DE CONTROL INTERNO

CAPITULO I
DISPOSICIONES GENERALES

Articulo 1º.
- Las disposiciones contenidas en las presentes normas señalan los estándares mínimos que deben ser observados por los organismos y entidades señalados en el artículo 2º, en el establecimiento, implantación, funcionamiento y evaluación de sus sistemas y mecanismos de control Entorno.

Articulo 2º
El Contralor General de la República, los titulares de los órganos de control externo de los Estados y Municipios y la máxima autoridad jerárquica de cada uno de los organismos y entidades a que se refieren los numerales 1 al 6 del artículo 5º de la Ley Orgánica de la Contraloría General de la República, son responsables por la aplicación de las presentes normas en sus respectivas estructuras de control interno.

CAPITULO II
DEL CONTROL INTERNO

Artículo 3º
El control Interno de cada organismo o entidad debe organizarse con arreglo a conceptos y principios generalmente aceptados de sistema y estar

69

constituido por las políticas y normas formalmente dictadas, los métodos y procedimientos efectivamente implantados y los recursos humanos, financieros y materiales, cuyo funcionamiento coordinado debe orientarse al cumplimiento de los objetivos siguientes:

Salvaguardar el patrimonio público.

Garantizar la exactitud, cabalidad, veracidad y oportunidad de la información presupuestaria, financiera, administrativa y técnica. Procurar la eficiencia, eficacia, economía y legalidad de los procesos y operaciones Institucionales y el acatamiento de las políticas establecidas por las máximas autoridades del organismo o entidad.

Articulo 4º.

Los objetivos del control interno deben ser establecidos para cada área o actividad del organismo entidad, y caracterizarse por ser aplicables, completas, razonables, Integrados y congruentes con los objetivos generales de la Institución.

Articulo 5º.

El control interno administrativo lo conforman las normas, procedimientos y mecanismos que regulan los actos de administración, manejo y disposición del patrimonio público y los requisitos y condiciones que deben cumplirse en la autorización de las transacciones presupuestarias y financieras.

## Articulo 6°

El control interno contable comprende las normas, procedimientos y mecanismos, concernientes a la protección de los recursos y a la confiabilidad de los registros de las operaciones presupuestarias y financieras, así como a producción de información atinente a las mismas.

## Articulo 7°.

El costo del control interno no debe exceder el resulte de la suma de los beneficios esperados de la función contralora. Son beneficios esperados del control Interno, en general, que incrementen la protección del Patrimonio público minimicen los riesgos de daños contra el mismo e incrementen su eficiente utilización.

## Artículo 8°

Los sistemas de control interno deben ser estructurados de acuerdo con las premisas siguientes:

a) Corresponde a la máxima autoridad jerárquica de cada organismo o entidad establecer, mantener y perfeccionar el sistema de control interno, y en general vigilar su efectivo funcionamiento. Asimismo, a los niveles directivos y gerenciales les corresponde garantizar el eficaz funcionamiento del sistema en cada área operativa, unidad organizativa, programa, proyecto, actividad u operación, de la cual sean responsables.

b) El sistema de control interno es parte de los sistemas financieros, presupuestarios, contables, administrativos y operativos del organismo o entidad y no un área independiente, individual o especializada.

c) Es responsabilidad del órgano de control interno del organismo o entidad, sin menoscabo de la que corresponde a la función administrativa, la revisión y evaluación del sistema de control Interno, para proponer a la máxima autoridad jerárquica las recomendaciones tendentes a su optimización y al incremento de la eficacia y efectividad de la gestión administrativa.

d) Sin menoscabo de que puedan aplicarse criterios técnicos de general aceptación relativos a la unidad e integridad de los procesos y a la forma unificada de su conducción gerencial, los deberes y responsabilidades atinentes a la autorización, ejecución, registro, control de transacciones y custodia del patrimonio público, deben mantener una adecuada y perceptible delimitación.

## Artículo 9°.

Los sistemas y mecanismos de control Interno deben estar sometidos a pruebas selectivas y continuas de cumplimiento y exactitud. Las pruebas de cumplimiento están dirigidas a determinar si dichos sistemas y mecanismos permiten detectar con prontitud cualquier desviación en el logro de las metas y objetivos programados, y en la adecuación de las acciones administrativas, presupuestarias y financieras a los procedimientos y normas prescritas. Las pruebas de exactitud están referidas a la verificación de la congruencia y consistencia numérica que debe existir en los registros contables entre si y en los estadísticos, y a la comprobación de la ejecución física de tareas y trabajos.

## Artículo 10.

Los niveles directivos y gerenciales de los organismos o entidades deben:

a) Vigilar permanentemente la actividad administrativa de las unidades, programas, proyectos u operaciones que tienen a su cargo;

b) Ser diligentes en la adopción de las medidas necesarias ante cualquier evidencia de desviación de los objetivos y metas programadas, detección de Irregularidades o actuaciones contrarias a los principios de legalidad, economía, eficiencia y la eficacia;

c) Asegurarse de que los controles internos contribuyan al logro de los resultados esperados de la gestión.

d) Evaluar las observaciones y recomendaciones formuladas por los organismos y dependencias encargados del control externo e interno, y promover la aplicación de las respectivas medidas correctivas.

## Articulo 11.

El órgano de control interno de los organismos o entidades debe estar adscrito al máximo nivel jerárquico de su estructura administrativa y asegurársele el mayor grado de independencia dentro de la organización, sin participación alguna en los actos típicamente administrativos u otros de índole similar.

Igualmente, la máxima autoridad jerárquica del organismo o entidad debe dotarlo de personal Idóneo y necesario, así como de razonables recursos presupuestarios, materiales y administrativos que le faciliten la efectiva coordinación del sistema de control Interno de la organización y el ejercicio de las funciones de vigilancia y fiscalización.

### Articulo 12.

Las funciones y responsabilidades del órgano de control interno deben ser definidas formalmentel mediante Instrumento normativo, por la máxima autoridad jerárquica de organismo o entidad, tomando en consideración a las disposiciones legales y reglamentarias vigentes y las normas, pautas e instrucciones que en materia de control dicten la Contraloría General de la República y demás órgano competentes para ello.

### Articulo 13.

Las funciones del órgano de control interno serán ejecutadas con base en un plan operativo anual, en cuya elaboración se aplicarán criterios de economía, objetividad oportunidad y de relevancia material, y se tomarán e consideración:

a) Los lineamientos establecidos en los planes nacionales estratégicos y operativos de control.

b) Los resultados de la actividad de control desarrollada en ejercicios anteriores.

c) Los planes, programas, objetivos y metas a cumplir por organismo o entidad en el respectivo ejercicio fiscal.

d) La situación administrativa, importancia, dimensión y área critica del organismo o entidad.

e) Las solicitudes de actuaciones y los lineamientos que formule la Contraloría General de la República, o cualquier organismo o entidad legalmente competente para ello.

f) Las denuncias recibidas.

g) Las propias recomendaciones, las que formulen las firmas de auditoría y los órganos de control externo.

### Artículo 14.

El órgano de control interno debe realizar la función de auditoría interna de conformidad con las disposiciones legales aplicables, las Normas

Generales de Auditoría de Estado prescritas por la Contraloría General de la República, las presentes Normas, otros instrumentos reglamentarios y las normas de auditoría de general y convencional aceptación.

## Artículo 15.

Las políticas que dicten los organismos o entidades deben definirse por escrito. Asimismo, deben adoptarse decisiones dirigidas a procurar la debida concordancia y adecuación de la organización con sus planes y programas, a establecer mecanismos para ejercer el control de las actividades de acuerdo con lo programado y a motivar al personal en la consecución de los objetivos y metas establecidos.

## Artículo 16.

La planificación debe ser una función institucional permanente, sujeta a evaluación periódica.

## Articulo 17.

Los planes, programas y proyectos de cada organismo o entidad deben estar en concordancia con los planes nacionales, estatales y municipales, y formularse con base a estudios y diagnósticos actualizados, teniendo en cuenta la misión de la Institución, sus competencias legales o estatutarias, el régimen jurídico aplicable y los recursos humanos, materiales y financieros que permitan el normal desarrollo de las actividades programadas.

## Articulo 18.

Los responsables de la ejecución de los planes, programas y proyectos, deben informar a los niveles superiores correspondientes acerca de la situación de los mismos, con indicación de las desviaciones ocurridas, sus causas, efectos, justificación y medidas adoptadas.

## Articulo 19

Las autoridades del organismo o entidad y en general los funcionarios y empleados bajo su supervisión, deben desempeñarse con arreglo a principios éticos y demostrada capacidad técnica e idoneidad en el cumplimiento de los deberes asignados.

Artículo 20

En los organismos y entidades deben estar claramente definidas, mediante normas e instrucciones escritas, las funciones de cada cargo, su nivel de autoridad, responsabilidad y sus relaciones jerárquicas dentro de la estructura organizativa, procurando que el empleado o funcionario sea responsable de sus actuaciones ante una sola autoridad.

Artículo 21.

El supervisor responsable de unidades, programas, proyectos u operaciones, debe comunicar claramente las funciones y responsabilidades atribuidas a cada supervisado, examinar sistemáticamente su trabajo y asegurarse que se ejecute conforme a las instrucciones dictadas al efecto.

Artículo 22.

Los manuales técnicos y de procedimientos deben ser aprobados por las máximas autoridades jerárquicas de los organismos y entidades. Dichos manuales deben incluir los diferentes pasos y condiciones de las operaciones a ser autorizadas, aprobadas, revisadas y registradas, así como lo relativo al archivo de la documentación justificativa que le sirva de soporte.

Artículo 23.

Todas las transacciones y operaciones financiera presupuestarias y administrativas deben estar respaldadas con la suficiente documentación justificativa. En este aspecto se tendrá presente lo siguiente:

Los documentos deben contener información completa exacta, archivarse siguiendo un orden cronológico u otro sistema de archivo que faciliten su oportuna localización, conservarse durante el tiempo estipulado legalmente.

Las autoridades competentes del organismo o entidad adoptarán las medidas necesarias para salvaguardar proteger los documentos contra incendios, sustracción cualquier otro riesgo, e igualmente, para evitar reproducción no autorizada.

Artículo 24.

El acceso a los registros y recursos materiales financieros debe limitarse a los funcionarios o empleados autorizados para ello, quienes estarán obligados a rendir cuenta de su custodia o utilización. La restricción del acceso los mismos dependerá de su grado de vulnerabilidad, del riesgo potencial de pérdidas, de la necesidad de reducir posibilidad de utilización no autorizada y de contribuir cumplimiento de las directrices de la organización.

## Articulo 25.

Se establecerá un adecuado sistema contabilidad para el registro oportuno y funcional operaciones financieras realizadas por la entidad u organismo, el cual deberá sujetarse a las Normas Generales Contabilidad del Sector Público prescritas por la Contraloría, a lo General de la República. Asimismo, los asientos deberán aprobados por un funcionario competente, con el propósito garantizar la correcta y exacta imputación en cada cuenta control.

## Articulo 26.

Todas las transacciones que ejecute un organismo o entidad y que produzcan Variaciones en sus activos, pasivos patrimonio, ingresos, gastos y, en general en cualesquiera las cuentas que conforman el sistema, deberán ser objeto registro contable en los libros."

It should be noted that it is not because of lack of laws that the fight against corruption is ineffective among Mercosur member countries. The ineffectiveness lies in the lack of political will since, regardless of the constant legislative changes, the legal-democrat principles remain unchanged.

Nowadays, the most evolved cycles of law are in no doubt as to the force of the principles. In fact, some call them principles of the norm, reason why they can be invoked in the name of morality, to govern the application of the sanction on the violator.

The principles of legality and morality are, in essence, dexterous tools for carving out substantial democracies with the help of the law.

Jessé Souza (2001, pp. 16-17, 78), in addressing democracy and its theoretical assumptions in our day, states:

> "In addition to elusive democracy, here are some modern and postmodern reflections:
> 'For Hobbes - and for all modernists after him - the individual is will, quite simply, while reason is simply the will's ability to solve problems. Disinhibited from

any 'sense of natural' or 'foreordained satisfaction of quest for essence,' the Hobbesian subject 'burst through modern Europe and spread throughout the world, planting urbanism, industrialism, and financial capitalism everywhere'

(...)

A member of a gang of thieves can express his power depending on his membership in that group, which can be directed to the common interest of the other members of the gang. However, he does so at the cost of suppressing his potentialities that can only come to terms through society in other groups. The gang cannot interact freely with other groups, but it can only act when it isolates itself from the other groups. It should prevent the conduction of all interests except those that characterize its uniqueness. On the other hand, a good citizen makes his performance as a member of a political group be enriching and enriched by participation in family, industrial, scientific, and artistic life. There is a free exchange relationship. The totality of the integrated personality is possible due to the dynamics of interaction between different groups and their values."

Yves Meny and Jean-Claude Thoenig also debated on the crisis of the modern state and its methods of political leadership. They have properly said that there is a plurality of actors and problems in society and that politics cannot be called "the evangelical truth." These authors offer us precious lessons in the following words (1992: 59, 102-103):

"La obra crucial de la literatura neo-marxista en este campo es el estudio de O'Connor sobre la crisis fiscal del Estado (O'Connor; 1973). La repercusión lie la obra fue considerable en Estados Unidos. Por primera vez, una interpretación marxista de la crisis fiscal era enunciada cuando las ciudades norteamericanas comenzaban a entrar en un marasmo financiero sin precedentes.

La teoría de la crisis fiscal de O'Connor propone interpretar las relaciones entre el Estado y la economía mediante el fenómeno de la socialización del capital; es decir, por el hecho de que las actividades de los capitalistas están cada vez más «socializadas» por el Estado. Esta socialización se hace de tres formas principales. En primer lugar, numerosos sectores económicos se benefician de subvenciones, transferencias o reducciones de los impuestos pilcadas por los contribuyentes. Ahora bien, la gran mayoría de estos recursos beneficia al capitalismo monopolista, tecnológicamente avanzado y gran consumidor de capitales. A esta primera forma, que O'Connor califica de socialización de la inversión, se suma la socialización del consumo, es decir, la provisión por el Estado de bienes colectivos (educación, salud, vivienda, cultura, etc.) Por último, una tercera forma, más compleja, que O'Connor califica de gastos sociales del capital, contribuye a mantener el control social del capitalismo. Estos tres modos de socialización del capital tratan de responder a las tres crisis que afectan al capitalismo contemporáneo: la caída de la tasa de beneficio, la insuficiencia del consumo y la crisis de legitimidad.

(...)

— Los métodos de conducción política (Offe, 1975). La clasificador distingue: 1) las prohibiciones y los estímulos; 2) la provisión de bienes servicios; y 3) los procedimientos. Esta clasificación ha sido revisada (Scharpf, 1976) distinguiendo de manera más detallada los instrumentos de influencia del Estado en: 1) prohibiciones; 2) estímulos; 3) bienes y servicios provistos por el Estado; 4) consecuencias provocadas por las infraestructuras públicas; y 5) procedimientos. ¿La acción pública es puntual o global en su realización? ¿Se dirige a las nuevas situaciones que se van a generar o se orienta hacia el tratamiento de las causas de disfunción social? ¿Se trata de erradicar problemas existentes o de evitar que aparezcan nuevos problemas

— Los instrumentos de gestión administrativa (Mayntz, 1978). Se pueden dividir en: 1) normas de prohibición y de requerimiento; 2) autorizaciones de actividades privadas; 3) transferencias financieras; 4)

estímulos financieros (subvenciones, etc.); y 5) provisión de bienes y servicios.

— La unción de conducción social del Estado (Hucke, 1980). Se despliega en los siguientes ámbitos: la regulación jurídica, la política social. ¡U conducción económica, las prestaciones simbólicas.

— Los instrumentos de gobierno (Hood, 1983). La autoridad pública dispone de dos mecanismos de control sobre la sociedad: los detectores (instrumentos para recoger información) y los realizadores (herramientas para generar impactos sobre la sociedad). Tiene a su disposición cuatro recursos: el «tesoro» (el dinero y otros recursos fungibles), la autoridad (la posesión de

(...)

poder legal o legítimo), la organización (la disposición de personal materiales, equipos), la «nodalidad» (el Estado se sitúa en el centro de un tejido social o de información). La combinación de estos dos mecanismos y de estos cuatro recursos genera los tipos específicos de las políticas públicas."

When dealing with the identification of needs that require specific public policies, the formulation of the problems that determine the priorities and finally the decision-making process, the same authors point out:

"Recientemente, aunque de manera tímida, los politólogos han tratado de comprender cómo emergen las políticas públicas. Para ello, se han planteado dos exigencias suplementarias:

— Tender un puente entre el estudio de lo que sucede en el seno del «sistema político» y el estudio de lo que ocurre en dé la «opinión pública», en sentido amplio. Esto significa especialmente que ya no se tomará como verdad evangélica que hay, por un lado, fenómenos puramente cognoscitivos y culturales en una población pasiva y marginada, y por otro lado, agentes activos que hacen política en una arena especializada, en el centro.

— Admitir, a título de hipótesis que debe verificarse, que en la sociedad existe una pluralidad de situaciones, de actores y de problemas. Corresponderá al analista constatar hasta qué punto esta pluralidad está efectivamente presente, si existen muchos escenarios políticos, muchas jerarquías de problemas. Si no es el caso, la pluralidad se esfuma, el encadenamiento es actores y los problemas se vuelve tan fuerte que se llega a una es-monolítica y jerárquica donde los más fuertes son siempre los más fuertes.

También puede formularse otra versión de esta exigencia metodológica.

(...)

3. La formulación de los problemas

La definición de un problema es un ámbito de controversia. Si hay controversia es porque:

— Tal formulación concreta implica consecuencias juzgadas inaceptables para una o varias de las partes implicadas: pueden verse recortadas ciertas ventajas, se imponen obligaciones.

— Las partes se sienten afectadas ante un problema que pone en cuestión principios fundamentales, valores absolutos; una especie de combate maniqueo entre el bien y el mal sin compromiso posible. Las posiciones son irreductibles, por lo que la formulación adopta un tono de guerra de religión.

— Hay refuerzos exteriores que pueden movilizarse si uno o varios actores públicos solicitan su apoyo. De ahí una función preventiva del conflicto, utilizada por los actores y los públicos que no están dispuestos a aceptar la llegada de esos refuerzos.

(...)

La decisión pública

Actuar es tomar decisiones. La decisión ocupa un lugar esencial en la jerarquía de los actos públicos, porque en ese preciso momento se juega la partida. Un responsable administrativo resuelve. Se seleccionan las soluciones. Una serie de acontecimientos derivan de ellas. Los interesados en la política pública considerada verán afectada su situación. El porvenir parece comprometido de manera irreversible.

En la vida concreta de la gestión pública todo concurre a la revaloración, cuando no a la sacralización, de la toma de decisiones. La Constitución o el organigrama precisan, a veces detalladamente, quién tiene derecho a firmar, en qué circunstancias, al final de qué trámites. El decisor final es la persona que cuenta, aquella cuyos humores, intereses y gestos se espían. Se le deben honores. Porque todo, en definitiva, descansa sobre sus espaldas y compromete su responsabilidad. En casa de la política, el decisor trabaja en el piso principal, como el capitán en un barco. Los consejeros o los expertos, si bien ayudan a decantar el problema y a generar alternativas, permanecen en la bodega.

El principio, el momento de la decisión representa el apogeo del trabajo político y administrativo. El resto parece secundario. Esta es, en parte, la razón por la cual, a los ojos del observador de la cosa pública, la decisión tiene valor privilegiado como reveladora del sistema político y, en consecuencia, de la estructura profunda de las comunidades y de las sociedades. Porque quien tiene la decisión ejerce el verdadero poder."

In politics, power is diffuse and the game is plural. Decisions are the result of a prior commitment between multiple and sometimes antagonistic forces, which is why the belief set forth by Skinner (2006: 441) states that *Suárez takes as his point of departure the fact that the crucial characteristics of men in the state natural are possessed by them all in common: they are all 'by nature free', all 'possess the use of their reason' and all 'have power over their own faculties.'*

Contemporary man is slowly transcending the old one who lived waiting on promises. Only gradually does it begin to cry out for material and immaterial achievements that traditional politics can no longer provide.

I sincerely believe that with the globalization of information that is growing at an alarming pace, we will migrate to the next phase in which the right of resistance will not only be understood, yet it will be exercised by our Mercosur peoples and, perhaps, even by the peoples in Africa, and peoples from other regions of the world.

It is up to us to take the helm of a new form of State in which democracy is substantial and politics revives its original ideal of promoting social justice.

# CHAPTER 5

# The Public Sector

The public sector is the portion of the economy controlled by the State administration, which aims to formulate public policies, regulate the market, and provide efficient and effective public services.

David Baigun and Nicolás García Rivas (2006: 87), in turn, define the scope of the adjective "public" as follows:

> "Y en este punto debe recordarse que lo público está constituido por aquellas cosas que pertenecen a todos, de las que todos toman parte y que, además, se desenvuelven en el espacio de la visibilidad. Público significa así lo que pertenece a todos, esto es, al pueblo, pero también lo que hace en público, a la vista de todos."

Aristotle says that a city is a set of citizens. These have always inhabited cities in search of the social dignity promised by the State.

The gradual awareness of the values of citizenship has enabled the historical man to distinguish between the public and the private, as João Gabriel Lima Teixeira (1986:54) points out:

> "If I take the classic authors - Marshall, Bendix or Tocqueville, who is the father of it all - everyone has an eminently urban discussion on citizenship. Marx himself, albeit with some disagreement with these classic authors, thought the problem of civil society basically as an urban society, where the field came to a halt.

To a certain extent, this connection is correct, because the city is the space where the distinction between public power and private power first manifests itself. Without this distinction between public and private, it is not possible to think citizenship as we understand it nowadays.

However, there is another historical reality, equally historically and empirically proven, another analysis that links citizenship precisely to labor relations in the rural world. For example, I think of Jerome Brum when he examines the end of the old European rural world. For him, the embryo of citizenship is exactly in the rural area; it is there that first appears a notion of contract that is fundamental to citizenship - and the peasant struggle to guarantee the minimum rights that launches the first idea of contractualism. Contractualism is the only element that cannot be lacking in the modern notion of citizenship, because it presupposes the fictitious legal equality of the contracting parties."

The State, as the manager of the public sector economy, has the duty to educate man for good government, as preached by Cicero and as Thomas Ransom Giles (1987:39) proclaimed in his *History of Education*, from which we transcribe the following excerpt:

"A sound State depends on the strengthening of the public spirit, and this, in turn, depends on citizens well raised by an educational process based on the strengthening of the moral character, the pure man of spirit and with a strong body, full of feelings of justice and public virtue. It is necessary to educate the citizen so that he is able to govern properly. This is done through the double process of literary instruction and personal development, plus plenty of practical experience. The Ciceronian ideal is the formation for effective action in real life. The program of studies recommended by him is aimed at utility in public and private enterprises, and not in empty knowledge."

Luís Roberto Gomes (2003: 107) correlates public sector and public policies as links of the same chain. Here is an excerpt from what the author says:

> "In the current stage of doctrinal and jurisprudence prospection on the matter, we think that public policy can be considered as the commissive or omissive conduct of the Public Administration, in a broad sense, aimed at achieving a program or goal established in a constitutional or legal norm, subject to wide judicial control, especially with regard to the efficiency of the means used and the evaluation of the results achieved (...) nowadays, the nomocratic state (= publisher of norms) is supplanted by the telocratic state, to which it is necessary to effectively implement the declarations contained in the norms, so that they go from the theoretical or formal plane to become suitable and operative public policies (...)And to say, the exigibility criterion goes from the simple statement expressed in the legal/constitutional norm in itself, to the field of the governmental program established in this norm, and for that reason it becomes paramount for the government the search of the means suitable for effectively implement the established objectives, which results that the inefficiency in the achievement of this requirement subjects the government to the control of its acts and omissions, and consequent accountability of its agents (MANCUSO, 1991, pp. 730-735)."

Julio E.S. Virgollini (2004: 105,114), agreeing with Jürgen Habermas, says that the State *"is the recognition that this society is entangled in an irremediable contradiction with itself."* He further points out:

> "Citando un texto de PAINE de 1776, HABERMAS refiere que "la sociedad es creada por nuestras necesidades, el Estado por nuestras debilidades. Cualquier estado de la sociedad es benéfico, el Estado, incluso en su mejor constitución, es un mal necesario (...) Los derechos naturales encuentran su real correspondencia en las leyes

del comercio y el tráfico; los individuos particulares obedecen éstas porque afectan inmediatamente a su interés y no porque el Estado imponga leyes formales bajo amenaza de castigo. Por esto, la praxis de un comercio libre y general garantizará los derechos humanos más rigurosamente que cualquier teoría que, habiéndose convertido en poder político sobre la opinión pública, dicte leyes y positivice así el derecho natural. La filosofía no necesita esforzarse por su realización.

Es pues, como se ve, toda una entera concepción filosófica vinculada con el derecho natural y con las bases ideológicas de la revolución estadounidense169 la que se encuentra detrás de la resistencia a aceptar el control del Estado en el control y la dirección de las actividades económicas, pues desde este punto de vista ellas pertenecen a la sociedad civil, y el poder del Estado sobre ellas no puede ser sino mínimo.

Pero la economía no es ciertamente fiel a sus bases filosóficas, y la esperanza de que la mano invisible del mercado y la concurrencia de todos los actores económicos en la libre persecución de sus fines particulares produjeran un estado equilibrado de bienestar en el que todos fueran beneficiados fue ilusoria. Los numerosos ejemplos de prácticas monopólicas, restricciones de acceso al mercado, acaparamiento de materias primas y productos, distorsión de precios y engaños frecuentes a los consumidores, que pusieron de manifiesto los *muckrakers* en los primeros años del siglo XX, bastan para demostrarlo."

When pondering about how the Mercosur states have treated their citizens, one sees that social dignity is the great promise of formal democracy that governs them.

It is well known that the Mercosur, African, and Asian States, as well as many in Oceania, have not yet paid the contributory effort of their citizens.

There is no doubt that a considerable part of the weakness of the State administration comes from the vampirism that corruption exercises over the public treasury.

# 5.1 – Corruption in the Public Sector

The responsibility for formulating public policies, regulating the market, and delivering efficient and effective public services makes the public sector the most responsible for the national development of the State administration.

This task is sometimes facilitated when the private sector acts as a partner and not as a predator of the public sector since development and corruption are antagonistic forces, as Mendieta (2000:143-144) asserts:

> "En países menos democráticos es frecuente que ciertas leyes violen normas y principios más elevados (por ejemplo los derechos humanos). Dado que las leyes y disposiciones oficiales siempre deben analizarse en función del sistema político, la corrupción destinada a eludir estas leyes inmorales puede encontrar una justificación moral o incluso puede ser necesaria. Como habremos de ver más adelante, no parece demasiado apropiado adoptar una óptica estrictamente legalista de la corrupción, sobre todo en relación con sistemas políticos no democráticos. Por lo tanto, siempre habrá que definir el interés común considerando las reglas formales de la función pública y el sistema político vigente; aunque esto último puede dar lugar a un sinnúmero de interpretaciones culturalistas y moralistas. (…)
>
> Es cierto que la descripción realizada requeriría muchos más detalles que explicaran mejor las transformaciones y sus causas, pero no es éste el lugar para realizar dicha labor. Lo que sí merece la pena destacar ahora es que, en el proceso de construcción de una Administración profesional en Estados Unidos o el

Reino Unido, respetuosa de la selección y carrera por mérito y capacidad y de las garantías de permanencia, un factor fundamental han sido los éxitos en los procesos de modernización social y económica. Y precisamente los procesos de modernización son una de las causas más importantes de corrupción en todos los países.

Ello es así por tres razones (Huntington, 1989). En primer lugar, la modernización implica un cambio en los valores básicos de la sociedad correspondiente. Segundo, la modernización crea nuevas fuentes de poder y riqueza, y los nuevos ricos y poderosos usan la corrupción para abrirse camino en el sistema político tradicional que intenta cerrarles las puertas. Es decir, que la expansión de la conciencia política y de la participación en un entorno no institucionalizado se conecta con la expansión de la corrupción. Tercero, la modernización implica la expansión de la autoridad gubernamental y la multiplicación de actividades sujetas a regulación pública. En consecuencia, la profesionalidad nació de la corrupción. Pero ¿cómo? Precisamente porque la corrupción permitió la generación de estructuras partidistas fuertes, estructuras que fueron poco a poco organizando y estructurando la participación política. El patronazgo permitió ir generando partidos que configuraron, a su vez, relaciones estables entre los grupos y pautas estables de autoridad reduciendo con ello las posibilidades de corrupción y violencia. La corrupción en esos casos históricos generó institucionalidad, lo cual fue clave para la reducción de la propia corrupción. Una vez que el sistema político estuvo institucionalizado, la presión social llevó a construir un servicio civil ya no dependiente de los partidos políticos, sino al servicio de los intereses generales. (…)

En países democráticos de larga tradición, el intento de reducir el peso de la burocracia e incrementar el papel de los políticos ha ido acompañado, a menudo, de claros incrementos de corrupción. Durante la Presidencia de

Reagan, los puestos de trabajo que podían ser ocupados por personas nombradas en función de criterios políticos —*political appointees*— aumentó notablemente, reduciéndose, en consecuencia, el papel y peso de la burocracia profesional. 'Curiosamente', la presidencia de Reagan fue una de las etapas más corruptas de la reciente historia norteamericana. La razón fundamental está en los diferentes estándares de moralidad que los burócratas profesionales y los políticos poseen (Frederickson, 1997)."

According to some political thinkers, corruption can be an ally to development to the extent that the corrupt official is willing to act in return for bribery in order to speed up projects and processes.

However, as we see it, corruption acts as a parasite that feeds on social development; a cancer cell that causes metastasis in the socio-economic body of the State.

David Baigun and Nicolas Garcia (2006: 87) have asserted that the archetype of corruption is the introduction of private interest as the reason or condition of public acts. Here is an illustrative excerpt:

> "La corrupción, cuyo arquetipo es la introducción de intereses privados como motivo o condición de los actos públicos, determina la confusión entre las esferas de lo público y lo privado. Esta confusión no es banal ni exenta de unas consecuencias que exceden al fenómeno considerado en su mera exterioridad. La circunstancia de que actos de la esfera pública se emitan o desplieguen sus efectos obedeciendo a intereses privados representa la destrucción de lo público como concepto y como patrimonio común de la ciudadanía."

José Ariel Núñez (2006: 21), when addressing the importance and influence of the public sector for the society, states:

"Nos hallamos frente a un sector como el gubernamental, que insume nada menos que el 25% promedio del Producto Nacional, que emplea entre el 15% y 20% de la población activa, que ejerce el control sobre los sectores de energía, transportes, comunicaciones, salud, educación, seguridad, defensa, etc., que aún atesora el 30% promedio del dominio de la propiedad inmueble y cuyo comportamiento administrativo fiscal regula y/o influencia el mercado financiero generando caídas o subas abruptas que conmocionan la economía toda."

When referring to corruption in the Public Sector, Núñez concludes that (2006:42):

> "En los países más pobres se encuentra generalizada y ostenta tasas altísimas, tanto en lo referido al índice general de corrupción de cada administración gubernamental, cuanto al porcentaje que se exige como costo del favoritismo, licencia o adquisición involucrada. En efecto, la tasa que una administración corrupta exige a la empresa privada va de un 20% a un
>
> 40% en los países en vías de desarrollo y desarrollados. Este costo es una sobrecarga de los presupuestos financieros gubernamentales que paga toda la población contribuyente.
>
> Hay quien dice que el control sobre la corrupción tiene un ideal: hallarle un límite promedio razonable, y ni siquiera extirparla por resultar esto imposible."

Martín Kanenguiser (2011: 21), in speaking of transverse corruption in the Argentine public sector, makes the following considerations:

> "La corrupción tal vez sea un caso emblemático por su predominio en la agenda pública durante los 90, frente a la apatía o el acostumbramiento que genera en la actualidad en la opinión pública, salvo escasas excepciones.
>
> La presidencia de Menem arrancó con el escándalo de sobornos del *Swiftgate* y el ingreso de dinero del narcotráfico, episodios protagonizados por integrantes de su familia política.
>
> La corrupción se ramificó a todo el gobierno, tanto a nivel individual – por otros casos de sobornos— como

institucional por los mecanismos poco transparentes con que se realizaron

las privatizaciones de las empresas de servicios en condiciones de clara desventaja para el país –como la dolarización de las tarifas— y con marcos regulatorios débiles.

El propio jefe de estado quedó salpicado por esa sensación de corrupción crónica inmortalizada en la frase 'Robo para la Corona', acuñada por su hábil y poco transparente negociador José Luís Manzano."

# 5.2 - Rupert Pritzl's Three Perspectives on Corruption

Rupert Pritzl (2000:63-65) outlines three different perspectives of corruption. Here they are:

1 - the first is the one in which the behavior of the public official departs from public interest;
2 - the second is the one in which the public official is a sort of "auctioneer" of public services, as we see in public biddings where probity is auctioned in exchange for bribes;
3 - the third perspective is directly related to probity as a duty that is raised from the exercise of the public function.

Here is the precious excerpt of Pritzl's thought:

"(1) Al definir la corrupción, los referentes del primer grupo destacan que dicha conducta se aparta del interés público ('public-interest-centered' definition). Intentan verificar si el funcionario efectivamente apunta al bien común durante el ejercicio de su cargo. El politólogo CARL JOACHIM FRIEDRICH explica la corrupción en los siguientes términos:

'...corruption can be said to exist whenever a power-holder... is by monetary or other rewards not legally provided for induced to take actions which favour whoever provides the reward and thereby does damage to the public and its interests.'

Es fundamental determinar quién define el 'interés público' y lo instituye con carácter obligatorio para todos, y cómo se establece la conducta que se aparta de esta norma dentro del ámbito político. El interrogante del 'whose norms set the criteria?', planteado por ARNOLD HEIDENHEIMER, MICHAEL JOHNSTON y VÍCTOR LEVINE, guarda una cierta similitud con la complicada pregunta acerca de una 'sociedad justa' y precisamente por esos mismos motivos no encuentra una respuesta unívoca en una sociedad libre y pluralista. Una réplica al estilo de 'the best opinion and morality of the time' no parece suficiente.

(2) A fin de evitar el aspecto normativo de la concepción del interés público, la segunda perspectiva de corrupción realiza una definición en la que destaca la modificación del mecanismo de coordinación. ROBERT TILMAN habla de un 'shift from mandatory pricing to a free-market-model,' mientras que NATHANIEL LEFF sencillamente se refiere a la corrupción como a una 'institución extra-legal' ('extra-legal institution'). Esta perspectiva de corrupción fue desarrollada fundamentalmente por autores cuyo objeto de estudio eran sociedades en las que prevalecían valores y conductas tradicionales y en las que no existían normas públicas formales. Por lo tanto, se establece una analogía directa entre una función pública y un trabajo en el sector privado, ya que ambos constituyen instrumentos para llevar a cabo objetivos personales y, sobre todo, para maximizar los ingresos privados. El historiador JACOB VAN KLAVEREN lo describe así:

'A corrupt civil servant regards his public office as a business, the income of which he will... seek to maximize. The office then becomes a 'maximizing unit'. The size of his income depends... upon the market situation and his talents for finding the point of maximal gain on the public's demand curve.'

Ambas analogías, la del cambio de coordenadas y la de la tendencia a maximizar los ingresos particulares, también quedan de manifiesto en el enfoque de LEFF, que considera al funcionario público corrupto como a una suerte de 'martillero para fines privados'. Durante el ejercicio de su cargo, el funcionario pone en marcha un proceso de ofertas por los beneficios del Estado y luego los distribuye según la voluntad individual de pago del potencial beneficiario. Así como la teoría microeconómica recurre a la imagen del martillero al estilo de LEÓN WALRAS, aquí se podría hablar del martillero de LEFF.

Es evidente que desde esta óptica resulta mucho más sencillo analizar el acto de corrupción. Una vez definido el funcionario público como martillero de LEFF, individuo caracterizado por una conducta de oferta y demanda económicamente racional, los instrumentos económicos pueden aplicarse con mayor facilidad. De hecho existen numerosos intentos que, por ejemplo, trasladan el enfoque de la teoría neoclásica de los precios a los actos de corrupción. No obstante, en una actitud improcedente, estos análisis excluyen los aspectos políticos y socioculturales relacionados con la corrupción y se rehúsan a considerar los factores dinámicos del proceso.

(3) La tercera definición encara la conducta del funcionario público que se aparta de su función o de sus deberes de funcionario ('public— office' o 'public-duty' definition) y, por lo tanto, puede ser calificada como una definición basada en los deberes. Considerando la mencionada imposibilidad de operacionalizar con suficiente exactitud el 'interés público', no sorprende que la definición más difundida sea la que destaca el concepto de 'función pública' ('public-office').

Dentro de este enfoque de corrupción, la concepción más aceptada se remite al sociólogo norteamericano JOSEPH S. NYE, cuya definición ya casi se ha convertido en 'clásica':

'Corruption is behavior which deviates from the formal duties of a public role because of private-regarding (personal, close family, private clique) pecuniary or status gains; or violates rules against the exercise of certain types of private-regarding influence. This includes such behavior as bribery (use of a reward to pervert the judgment of a person in a position of trust); nepotism (bestowal of patronage by reason of ascriptive relationship rather than merit); and misappropriation (illegal appropriation of public resources for private-regarding uses).'

Además de los tres elementos centrales de corrupción destacados por SENTURIA, esta definición clásica de NYE permite distinguir las tres formas más usuales de corrupción. (PRITZL, Rupert: Corrupción y Rentismo en América Latina. Buenos Aires: CIEDLA, Fundación Honrad Adenauer, 2000. p. 63-65.)"

Corruption in the public sector, given the growing and worrying poverty of the world, has already been the subject of international conventions, such as the United Nations Convention Against Corruption (UNCAC), which calls on States members to develop means to prevent corruption of their employees.

This is an excerpt from the UNCAC, quoted in the *Oficina anticorrupción. Ministerio de Justicia y Derechos Humanos de Argentina* (2004: 27-28, 47):

"El artículo 7 "Sector Público" establece:

1. Cada Estado Parte, cuando sea apropiado y de conformidad con los principios fundamentales de su ordenamiento jurídico, procurará adoptar sistemas de convocatoria, contratación, retención, promoción y jubilación de empleados públicos y, cuando proceda, de otros funcionarios públicos no elegidos, o mantener y fortalecer dichos sistemas. Éstos:

   a) Estarán basados en principios de eficiencia y transparencia y en criterios objetivos como el mérito, la equidad y la aptitud;
   b) Incluirán procedimientos adecuados de selección y formación de los titulares de cargos públicos que se consideren especialmente

vulnerables a la corrupción, así como, cuando proceda, la rotación de esas personas a otros cargos;

c) Fomentarán una remuneración adecuada y escalas de sueldo equitativas, teniendo en cuenta el nivel de desarrollo económico del Estado Parte;

d) Promoverán programas de formación y capacitación que les permitan cumplir los requisitos de desempeño correcto, honorable y debido de sus funciones y les proporcionen capacitación especializada y apropiada para que sean más conscientes de los riesgos de corrupción inherentes al desempeño de sus funciones. Tales programas podrán hacer referencia a códigos o normas de conducta en las esferas pertinentes.

2. Cada Estado Parte considerará también la posibilidad de adoptar medidas legislativas y administrativas apropiadas, en consonancia con los objetivos de la presente Convención y de conformidad con los principios fundamentales de su derecho interno, afín de establecer criterios para la candidatura y elección a cargos públicos.

3. Cada Estado Parte considerará asimismo la posibilidad de adoptar medidas legislativas y administrativas apropiadas, en consonancia con los objetivos de la presente Convención y de conformidad con los principios fundamentales de su derecho interno, para aumentar la transparencia respecto de la financiación de candidaturas a cargos públicos electivos y, cuando proceda, respecto de la financiación de los partidos políticos.

4. Cada Estado Parte, de conformidad con los principios fundamentales de su derecho interno, procurará adoptar sistemas destinados a promoverla transparencia y a prevenir conflictos de intereses, o a mantener y fortalecer dichos sistemas.

Virgollini (2004:239-241) addressing white-collar crimes of corruption, says:

"De esta manera, el logro de los favores, las complacencias o las protecciones de los poderes públicos fueron hasta ahora presentados como el modo por el cual los delincuentes (de cuello blanco o del crimen organizado) prosperaban o hacían prosperar su negocio.

Los ejemplos son variados: el dictado de leyes favorables a cierto sector empresario, el otorgamiento de subsidios o de regímenes fiscales, aduaneros o de cualquier otra índole, el desfavorecimiento de sectores o de grupos en concurrencia, la debilidad en la investigación y la lenidad en el juzgamiento de las infracciones, el énfasis puesto en políticas no estrictamente penales fueron, de manera general, algunos de los trazos que caracterizaron el delito de cuello blanco y que culminaron con su relativa inmunidad a los procesos de criminalización o de reprobación social. Aunque con algunas particularidades derivadas sobre todo del imaginario social y de las representaciones habituales sobre la cuestión, el crimen organizado se supo hacer beneficiario de favores parecidos, y cada vez más cuanto mayor era su 'inserción en la economía legal.

En la confusión existente entre la economía legal y la economía ilegal, y en la correlativa superposición y confusión entre el crimen económico o de cuello blanco y el crimen organizado, el recurso a la corrupción constituye una especie de técnica compartida, de *know how* comunitario. Todos ellos han sobornado a los políticos, a los funcionarios, a los jueces y a los policías y en general los contactos para desarrollar estos métodos son más sofisticados, costosos, discretos y seguros a medida de que se eleva en la jerarquía social y la índole y la importancia de los negocios requieren cada vez más de las mediaciones de la política. (…)

Y tampoco lo es el hecho de que se trata de un género de episodios que de alguna manera constituye un punto de encuentro, o más bien un ancho campo común que hermana al delito de cuello blanco con el crimen organizado, y que está presente en la mayoría de las variantes de cada uno de ellos. Porque de la misma manera que lo hemos señalado respecto de las relaciones existentes entre el delito de cuello blanco y el crimen organizado, la superposición nunca es completa: es frecuente que estos dos géneros recurran a la corrupción, pero a veces no, y para algunos de sus actores el recurso a la violencia, al engaño o al fraude les resulta suficiente."

The public sector from the political-juridical point of view is the State administration itself with its virtues and weaknesses. It is directly responsible for the government and material and cultural development of the nation and almost always has the material and human resources for such a task.

Failure to meet public needs due to a lack of resources is acceptable, but not to do so because of a lack of preventive and repressive fight against corruption is to deny its own reason for existing, a hypothesis in which the Right of Resistance can and should be exercised by the community, in order to restore the equality of the parties in the Social Contract.

# CHAPTER 6

# The Private Sector

Private sector is the portion of the economy that is not under direct control of the State. It was the first sector to be structured, and as such, it became the most experienced in the generation of wealth and accumulation of profit.

In fact, the private sector is not the focus of this work, but we cannot fail to mention it given the intrinsic relationship between active and passive corruption that binds both sectors bilaterally.

David Baigun (2006: 74) makes the following reflection on conflicts of interest in the private sector:

> "Los conflictos de intereses en el sector privado ponen de manifiesto la fatal atracción del poder económico frente a los tradicionales criterios de honorabilidad en el campo profesional y laboral, frente a la ética de los negocios."

The report from *Oficina Anticorrupción del Ministerio de Justicia y Derechos Humanos* in Argentina (2004: 70-71), when commenting on the *Convención de Naciones Unidas Contra La Corrupción*, points out:

> "(...) Resulta claro que los problemas de corrupción no se dan solamente en el ámbito de lo público; la importancia e incidencia de los fraudes y corrupción en el sector privado son actualmente ampliamente reconocidos. La discusión, sin embargo, se refirió más a la pertinencia de incluir disposiciones por las cuales los gobiernos que

ratifiquen la Convención se obligarán a establecer medidas de prevención referidas a las empresas privadas, aún en relaciones que no involucran sujetos públicos y sobre las reales posibilidades de hacer efectivas esas medidas. Finalmente, se impuso la idea de que, dado el enorme impacto que la corrupción a nivel privado tiene sobre el conjunto de la sociedad, resultaba adecuado incorporar estas disposiciones."

# 6.1 - State Takeover by the Private Sector

Corruption in the private sector constitutes a more concerning matter when it aims to takeover and imprison the State. This is why international bodies have decided to issue anti-corruption rules to signatories of treaties and conventions.

When the private sector makes contracts, works, services, purchases, concessions, permits, and state authorizations hostage of acts or system of corruption, it ends up bleeding the public coffers and undermining public policies of inclusion of the needy.

The report of the Argentine Anti-Corruption Office (2004: 70-71), in dealing with conflicts between the public and private sectors, states:

"En el ámbito relacionado con los conflictos de intereses, podemos mencionar como efecto notorio de las privatizaciones la concentración de mucho poder en manos de ciertos grupos económicos. Esta concentración pudo haberse tornado, en algunas áreas, en lo que algunos autores denominan como 'captura del Estado'. Según la noción más extendida de 'captura del Estado', se asocia esa práctica con la voluntad de actores del sector privado de influir en la formulación de las reglas de juego básicas (bajo la forma de leyes, decretos, regulaciones, etc.) mediante pagos privados ilícitos a los funcionarios encargados de definir esas reglas. En las condiciones particulares que el proceso de privatizaciones de empresas públicas tuvo en Argentina, la 'captura del Estado' no se limitaría meramente a la generación de las reglas de juego por medio de pagos, sino-que asume otras características: los grupos económicos beneficiados por la distribución de empresas en el proceso privatizador tuvieron la oportunidad de influir en los entes de regulación de servicios públicos mediante la ubicación en puestos estratégicos de agentes relacionados a esos grupos de manera de establecer mecanismos permanentes por medio de los cuales la influencia de esos grupos se consolidara."

Rupert Pritzl (2000: 66-67), in his work *Corrupción y Rentismo en América Latina,* points out that corruption in the private sector produces less damage because control systems are more effective and the hierarchy less stratified. After all, the impoverishment of the individual is less shocking than the impoverishment of the collectivity caused by the dilapidation of the common good. Here is what Pritzl says:

"Las conductas corruptas pueden manifestarse tanto en administraciones del sector público como del sector privado. No obstante, hay claros indicios de que el nivel de corrupción en el sector público supera en forma considerable a la dimensión alcanzada en el ámbito privado. Las razones hay que buscarlas fundamentalmente en los aspectos institucionales y en los tipos de conducta, que marcan evidentes diferencias entre ambas administraciones:

Las organizaciones privadas, por ejemplo, cuentan con mejores posibilidades de control e incentivo dentro de la propia organización, presentan objetivos más definidos y mejor estructurados y disponen de una autoridad menos fragmentada, además de destacarse por un reclutamiento más eficiente y una remuneración acorde con el rendimiento evidenciado. En vista de estos argumentos, EDWARD BANFIELD postula que la conducta corrupta se manifiesta con mayor frecuencia en la administración pública que en la administración de organizaciones privadas, y que en consecuencia el nivel de corrupción es mayor en las administraciones públicas. (…) "Corruption is a consequence of discretionary political authority."

Another issue that deserves to be addressed at the level of national and international legislation is the application of the *persecutio criminis* and the *jus puniendi* of the State against the author of the act of corruption because the differentiated treatment between the individual and the public official becomes a privilege for one in detriment of the other.

We believe that the monist theory adopted by the Penal Code of Brazil is the most appropriate as a criterion of punishment to those who practice acts of corruption since it ensures that the one who contributes to the crime in any way focuses on the penalties he commits to the extent of his guilt.

It should be noted that all the subjects who participate in the criminal act account for the same act, to the extent of their guilt, sharing the responsibility between authors, co-authors, and participants in the conjecture of people.

Julio E.S. Virgolini (2004: 105) in his work *Crímenes excelentes: Delitos de cuello blanco, crimen organizado y corrupción*, affirms that the differentiated treatment diminishes the strength and effectiveness of the law:

> "La afirmación original se debe a SUTHERLAND, quien señalo que lo que ocultaba la delincuencia en la conducta de las corporaciones que fueron el objeto de su investigación era el hecho de la aplicación diferencial de la ley, ciado que eliminaba o por lo menos minimizaba el estigma del delito, y que esta aplicación diferencial se explicaba por tres factores: el estatus del hombre de negocios, la tendencia hacia el no castigo y el resentimiento relativamente desorganizado del público hacia los delitos de cuello blanco."

This structure of economic law already allows the penalization of the juridical person, surpassing the Savignian theory that *societas delinquere non potest*, as emphasized by Virgolini (2004: 127-128):

> "El derecho criminal considera al hombre natural, es decir, un ser libre, inteligente y sensible: la persona

jurídica por el contrario, se encuentra despojada de esos caracteres, siendo sólo un ser abstracto capaz de poseer, y que el derecho criminal no podría mezclarse en su esfera de acción; la realidad de su existencia se funda sobre las determinaciones de un cierto número de representantes que, en virtud de una ficción, son consideradas como sus propias determinaciones; y una representación parecida, que excluya la voluntad propiamente dicha, puede tener efecto en cuanto al derecho civil, nunca en cuanto al penal."

In the infinity of controls there is no control at all, just as the infinity of laws does not serve the promotion of substantial justice.

The final result of this exacerbation of laws or controls that exist among members of Mercosur is impunity. This permissive state discredits the norm and makes the democratic state a justification of formal democracy that interests those who use their positions, jobs, functions, and public terms as a means of personal fulfillment.

# 6.2 - The Privatization of the Law

Another dangerous aspect of the lack of a fight against corruption in the private sector is the privatization of the law, which occurs when members of this sector manipulate it, either by economic pressure or by electing representatives to act in branches of the government in order to benefit from the State.

This is how Virgolini (2004: 261-262, 263) presents the subject:

"La ley y el Estado se han convertido así en un sistema de recursos públicos generadores de beneficios desiguales, que se derraman de modo no público sobre grupos selectos de particulares de una manera contradictoria con la pretensión de generalidad e impersonalidad de la ley que los regula. El diagrama requiere privilegiar las relaciones personales clandestinas por sobre los derechos impersonales que consagra el sistema legal formal propio del Estado de derecho.

De este modo, tanto la ley en sí misma, como medio de vinculación igualitaria entre los ciudadanos, como los derechos y beneficios que de ella se esperan, pasan a ser un recurso que de público en su origen y en su concepción originarias se privatiza y que es empleado de modo excluyente por quienes tienen u obtienen ese acceso privilegiado que otorga la corrupción. (…)

El empleo privado de la ley es doblemente excluyente: no sólo excluye a los ciudadanos comunes de las ventajas que el Estado les puede brindar en el sentido acotado de actores económicos, sino que también los priva de la disponibilidad de la ley, esto es, de la condición sobre la que reposa su misma calidad de ciudadanos."

It is not surprising that corruption harms all sectors of the economy, which is why a preventive and repressive administrative and criminal policy is necessary, as Baigun (2006: 445-446) points out:

"En el derecho de sociedades se viven tiempos de cambio. El ideario que impulsa los movimientos legislativos y que viene gestándose desde finales de los años setenta es el denominado *corporate governance*. El terreno para que este programa normativo, oriundo de los Estados Unidos, haya germinado y crecido con vigor en Europa ha sido abonado por un compuesto en el que se dan cita la globalización y, en concreto, la mundialización de los mercados financieros; el conjunto de crisis empresariales que han sacudido la economía americana en el cambio de siglo; la denominada sociedad de riesgos y, por qué no, una concientización global acerca de problemas sociales como el medio ambiente y la protección de los derechos humanos. El objeto de estas líneas es analizar este escenario, los retos que implica para el derecho, las estrategias jurídicas que se están desarrollando para afrontarlo, para a continuación detenerse en el análisis de las consecuencias que de todo ello se derivan para el derecho penal de la empresa.

En concreto, el argumento de fondo de este trabajo podría ser compendiado del siguiente modo: el desarrollo de la economía capitalista que se corresponde con la sociedad globalizada y del riesgo requiere una nueva estrategia penal. La piedra angular en la que ésta debe descansar consiste en la necesidad de que las empresas colaboren con el estado con el fin de asegurar la eficacia del derecho. Si las grandes empresas multinacionales y las sociedades cotizadas, no se convierten en una suerte de agentes del estado, comprometiéndose seriamente en la prevención y sardón de los comportamientos desviados que puedan realizar sus empleados y directivos, gran parte de las normas de conducta cuya eficacia trata de asegurar mediante el derecho penal económico serán papel mojado. Esta alianza entre los agentes del capitalismo y el estado es parte del ideario de la *corporate governance*, como resulta patente de los índices de los códigos de conducta o códigos éticos que hasta hace poco han sido la principal base normativa del gobierno corporativo. En todos ellos, si bien con distinta intensidad, se recogen como aspectos la prevención; sanción, por parte de la empresa, de un buen número de comportamientos delictivos (corrupción, explotación de trabajadores, no discriminación, medio ambiente, etc.)."

Rupert Pritzl (2006: 126-127) lists a series of dire consequences arising from the privatization of the State by the private sector. Here is an excerpt from his reflections on this theme:

"Los cambios de conducta resultantes de esta 'privatización del Estado' pueden resumirse en los siguientes términos:

Se obstruye intencionalmente la gestión administrativa y se demoran innecesariamente las actuaciones con el propósito de exigir a los afectados una suerte de canon que acelere los trámites o eluda ciertas vías burocráticas.

—Los burócratas buscan acumular en su persona todas las competencias posibles para volverse 'indispensables' en una gran cantidad de diferentes ámbitos.

— Se atomizan artificialmente las estructuras administrativas y se les resta transparencia para aumentar las oportunidades de soborno.

— Se amplían las injerencias del Estado y se extiende su marco de competencia a cada vez más sectores de la vida económica y social.

— Se privilegian las mega-inversiones y, en particular, los proyectos de infraestructura intensivos en capitales por sobre los trabajos de mantenimiento intensivos en mano de obra.

— Se privilegian las obras con tecnología de vanguardia, intensiva en capital, frente a obras estándar con tecnología intensiva en mano de obra y adaptada a las necesidades locales."

The private sector needs to be responsible for the common good. In this globalized world, in which private and public activities are completely determinant of the substantiality of democracy and life on the planet, responsibilities must be shared equally in order to generate social well-being, without which the development and balance between the rich and the poor are increasingly threatened.

Extreme poverty is a reflection of the extreme injustice promoted by our current formal democracies that have already made one of the dishes of the scale of social equilibrium so low that it is close to touching the bottom of the abyss.

It is no longer the yellow light that is lit on the panel of social dignity. We have already passed the red light. I am sure that in many parts of the world poverty and extreme injustice will start to take its toll.

# CHAPTER 7

# The Costs of Corruption

Daniel Artana repudiates the saying that bribe is the oil that makes the administrative machine work. He also says that it is easier to be corrupt in a major work of infrastructure than in the performance of 50 small works.

Artana is irreproachable when he speaks against corruption and says (1998: 90-91):

> "Aquella frase de que la coima es el aceite del sistema, no sólo es errada, sino que la corrupción tiene altos costos y efectos devastadores para el sistema. El primer costo es que la corrupción reduce el crecimiento económico. Hay estudios internacionales, hechos por el FMI, por ejemplo, que muestran que en los países más corruptos, el crecimiento es más bajo. ¿Y por qué pasa esto? La corrupción distorsiona las decisiones en materia de inversión pública. Es más fácil ser corrupto en una nueva gran obra de infraestructura y no en el mantenimiento de 50 pequeñas obras, ya que es más difícil estar en connivencia con 50 empresas simultáneamente. Así, se sesga la inversión en contra del mantenimiento de la infraestructura y a favor de hacer nuevas obras. Esto sin contar el lado político. A los funcionarios les gusta inaugurar grandes obras y no anunciar que la ruta está bien mantenida, porque con eso no se puede cortar ninguna cinta. Otro aspecto de la digitación de inversiones es que los proyectos malos pueden reemplazar a proyectos

buenos, simplemente porque la empresa que está atrás del proyecto malo tiene más capacidad de corromper y de entrar en una transa ilegítima con el funcionario."

David Baigun and Nicolás García Rivas (2006: 40) are some of the authors who denounce the numbers of the damage caused by economic crimes in Argentina. They say:

"Ahora bien, de acuerdo con los cálculos efectuados, el perjuicio estimado para el período 1980-2005 asciende a 10.144 millones de dólares. Sobre el total de esta cifra, sólo en el fuero federal el perjuicio producido por los delitos económicos asciende a 8.724 millones de dólares."

On February 8, 2011, official corruption in Argentina was cause for such concern that the US Embassy in Buenos Aires sent more than one hundred confidential messages alerting to the fragility of the judicial system and, consequently, to the impunity of the offenders.

Reports on the lack of political will to combat corruption, which has been generalized throughout the government Branches, especially the judiciary, and also the police, and the political class.

The newspaper *El País* reported:

"La renuncia del fiscal argentino anticorrupción Manuel Garrido, en marzo de 2009, alegando la imposibilidad de cumplir con su trabajo, maniatado por restricciones normativas, fue recibida con desagrado por la legación diplomática norteamericana. La embajada había seguido atentamente las investigaciones de Garrido sobre el sospechoso incremento patrimonial del matrimonio Kirchner y de funcionarios del entorno presidencial. "Los recientes movimientos del gobierno argentino socavan la independencia y la eficacia de los organismos con jurisdicción sobre casos de corrupción", condenó la embajada."(http://internacional.elpais.com/internacional/2011/02/08/actualidad/1297119616_850215.html. acesso em 08.12.2013)

In Brazil, the Getúlio Vargas Foundation stated that corruption cost was of US$3.5 billion to public coffers annually.

Here is the text that brings other important considerations, such as the fact that data from the NGO Transparency International show that Brazil's Corruption Perceptions Index is similar to that of countries like Belize, Sri Lanka, Peru, Kuwait, and Colombia:

"A Brazilian pays dearly for the increase of corruption in the country. According to a study done by the coordinator of the School of Economics of São Paulo, Fundação Getúlio Vargas (FGV), Marcos Fernandes, the loss of productivity caused by public fraud in Brazil reaches $3.5 billion per year. 'Just as well-structured roads and ports improve Brazil's productivity, inefficient institutions diminish the nation's gain,' says Fernandes.

He explains that the loss was calculated on the basis of World Bank data on education and investment from 109 countries, as well as corruption perception figures from the nongovernmental organization Transparency International. In the evaluation of the FGV professor - who today launches the book *Ética e Economia,* in São Paulo -, with the poor quality of laws, governance, and the business environment, companies hesitate to invest in the country and stop creating jobs and income for the society. Just to have an idea of what the loss of productivity caused by corruption in Brazil means, it is enough to compare the volume of money committed by the government in the Department of Transport. Up to August, about 5.3 billion Brazilian Reais were spent in transportation infrastructure works, such as roads, waterways, railroads, and ports - well below the annual productivity loss estimated at $3.5 billion, or R$7,5 billion Brazilian Reais at a R$2.17 conversion rate.

Fernandes adds that only in two recent scandals in Brazil's history - the super-billing of the Regional Labor Court (TRT) of São Paulo by Judge Nicolau dos Santos Neto and that of the leeches - the population lost about US$ 150 million. 'With this money, it would be possible to build 200,000 houses and house to 800,000 people,' the professor calculates. According to him, much of money that could be invested in the country's precarious infrastructure is diverted by corruption. As a result, the state loses its strength and its investment policies are weakened. This can be seen in the 2006-2007 Global

Competitiveness Index of the World Economic Forum. Figures released last week show that Brazil has fallen nine places in the international ranking, from 57th to 66th, falling below the other countries that form the so-called BRIC (Russia, India, and China). According to the Forum, Brazil's performance is due in particular to two factors: macroeconomic and institutional indicators. 'Corruption has serious effects on market competition,' said Claudio Weber Abramo, Executive Director of Transparency Brazil.

According to him, the effect on the population is distressing, since less investments mean less employment, income, and worsening of the well-being of the population. 'The social cost is huge because it deprives people of a better quality of life and freedom of choice,' says Fernandes. Economist Reinaldo Gonçalves, professor at the Federal University of Rio de Janeiro (UFRJ), adds that corruption increases the risk and uncertainty in the country's business environment. 'To protect it, the prices of goods and services end up embedding the cost of corruption, as if it were a tax,' he says. For the professor, besides increasing the uncertainties, public frauds raise the opportunistic practices. 'As some commit unlawful acts and are not punished, others also adopt corrupt weapons to compete.' In his assessment, there is a systemic fragility in Brazil, a process of 'Africanization'. Data from the NGO Transparency International show that Brazil's Corruption Perceptions Index is similar to that of countries like Belize, Sri Lanka, Peru, Kuwait, and Colombia. The safest countries are Finland, Denmark, Singapore, and Switzerland. The worst in public fraud are Bangladesh, Paraguay, and Indonesia. In the evaluation of the professor of Ethics and Political Philosophy of Unicamp, Roberto Romano, one of the problems that raise the index of corruption in Brazil is the number of mediators in the system. From the federal government to the destination, the money goes through several hands, which facilitates fraud, he argues. 'The result is the inequality between the regions and the lack of competitiveness of the Brazilian product. If you have no added value, especially cutting-edge, what do you have to offer? Nothing', the professor points out.

But there is a light at the end of the tunnel, experts argue. One alternative is to stop treating corruption as the cause of morality. For Abramo, it originates in fragile administrative institutions and practices. 'In Brazil, governments can nominate to office randomly in exchange for parliamentary support. This needs to be changed,' he says indignantly, calling for the creation of conflict-of-interest management policies. 'Certainly you do not fight corruption by saying that it is ugly.' Gonçalves, from the FGV, believes that the establishment of mechanisms that allow public oversight of the government budget would already contribute to reducing fraud. 'Transparency is needed. If you make everything electronic, you can check the progress of the processes, service purchase agreements, etc.' But this must be intelligible. There is no point in having data if you cannot read it, he warns. 'Added to this is the need to reduce bureaucracy and to approve more rational laws.'"

The $ 3.5 billion seems unbelievable. In any country in the world, it is notorious that data pertaining to deviations of money and revenues from public coffers released by the public sector and by the private sector or third sector are mismatched.

What makes the difference is that in some countries where the educational process of the population is more effective, the control is more rigid and the data a little closer to reality.

In 2010, the Federation of Industries of São Paulo (Fiesp) reported that deviations exceed 69 billion Brazilian Reais. Here is the text:

> "The price of corruption costs Brazil between R$ 41.5 and R$ 69.1 billion Brazilian Reais per year. The estimate is from a study released today (13) by the Federation of Industries of São Paulo (Fiesp).
>
> According to the report *Corruption: Economic Costs and Combat Proposals*, the cost of corruption represents between 1.38% and 2.3% of the Gross Domestic Product (GDP).

Money, if invested in education, for example, could increase the number of students enrolled in the public elementary school network from 34.5 million to 51 million, in addition to improving the living conditions of the Brazilian people.

'The extremely high cost of corruption in Brazil impairs the increase in per capita income, growth and competitiveness of the country, compromises the possibility of offering better economic conditions and social welfare to the population and to companies better infrastructure conditions and more stable business environment, 'says the Fiesp study.

The report also points out that if the budget deviation in the country were smaller, the number of hospital beds in public hospitals could rise from 367,397 to 694,409.

The deviant money could also build more than 2.9 million households and bring basic sanitation to more than 23.3 million households.

For the area of infrastructure, the report estimates that if there was not so much corruption, 277 new airports could be built in the country.

The precariousness of the terminals is one of the biggest problems for the 2014 World Cup in Brazil.

The study also reveals, citing information from the nongovernmental organization Transparency International, that the country managed to reduce corruption, but it was not enough to get it out of the 75th place in 2009 in a ranking of 180 countries." (http://www.brasileconomico. com.br/noticias/corrupcao-no-brasil-custa-ate-r-691- bilhoes-por-ano_82676.html. Retrieved on 12/08/2013.)"

However, the disagreements about the truth of stratospheric deviations do not stop there because for the UN the annual values exceed 200 billion Brazilian Reais. Here is the text:

"In addition to having occupied, in 2012, the position of number 73 in the list of the most corrupt countries in the world, which is measured according to the population perception, it is diverted, according to the United Nations Development Program, UN responsibility, at least $ 200 billion Brazilian Reais per year in Brazil (data for 2012).

In a meeting promoted by the body and held in November 2012 in Brasilia, fifty experts were summoned to discuss the problem and possible anti-corruption practices.

The amount is higher than the sum of the amounts spent on health and education, which, together, are responsible for the expenditure of R$140 billion Brazilian Reais. That is, if there were no corruption, the amounts invested in these sectors could double and there would still be R$60 billion Brazilian Reais left.

According to Transparency International, in a more recent study, the country slightly improved its position, reaching the position of number 69. However, it is worth noting that this does not necessarily mean 'improvement': the index measures the perception, not covering the actual, real, and comprehensive levels of corruption.

It is also worth noting that such values do not include the misuse of public money, i.e. expenditure on fake programs, stationary works, concerts, bread and circus policy, expenses for the construction of stadiums, among other questionable policies (http://www.folhapolitica.org/2013/06/corruptos-desviam-200-bilhoes-por-ano.html. Retrieved12/03/2013)"

On July 17, 2013, an important Brazilian communication vehicle promoted a debate among specialists in public resources deviation when Professor Marco Antonio Villa said that it is almost impossible to quantify deviations because the control mechanisms are not enough. (http://jovempan.uol.com.br/noticias/brasil/qual-o-custo-da-corrupcao-especialistas-avaliam-o-impacto-deste-crime-no-brasil.html. Retrieved on 7.12.2013)

Although we disagree strongly when Marco Antonio Villa says that the mechanisms of control are insufficient, since we have demonstrated the contrary in this work, we agree that it is difficult to reach a real quantification of the deviations of public money and revenues. This is also because it is not in the interest of the political class that the people have access to the truth.

In the same interview, Claudio Abramo, Director of Transparency Brazil, reveals that the Brazilian State itself is in charge of facilitating the path of the corrupt when it allows the appointment of adventurers for commissioned offices. It even makes a comparison of the same practice with other nations and the result is:

1)  The United States, which has a gigantic administrative machine, appoints 9,000 commissioned agents;
2)  France appoints 500 commissioners;
3)  Germany appoints 500 commissioners;
4)  England appoints 300 commissioners;
5)  THE BRAZILIAN FEDERAL GOVERNMENT APPOINTS 21 THOUSAND ADVENTURERS FOR POSITIONS IN THE OFFICES and these numbers are identical in the state and municipal administrations. For example, only the Federal District appoints 20,000 commissioners.

The chief economist of FIEL - *Fundación de Investigaciones Económicas Latinoamericana* published the article *"Los costos económicos de la corrupción"* in which he says that in Mexico, bribery is seen as the "oil of the system."

He argues that corruption produces economic, social, and ethical costs. In his own words, he states:

> "Un amigo mexicano me decía una vez: "La coima es el aceite del sistema" y aunque cueste aceptarlo, este argumento es común en economías latinas como la nuestra. Es el mismo razonamiento que sustenta el libro de Armando de Soto, El otro sendero, donde se justifica la corrupción con frases como: "Algunas regulaciones son tan disparatadas que la gente las saltea y de esa forma consigue evitar los costos de la regulación". Es la misma teoría de algunos economistas –quienes han llegado a escribir trabajos sobre esto— que sostienen que si la evasión fiscal fuera pareja, si todos evadiéramos lo mismo, en realidad no habría costos por evasión fiscal. Pero las cosas no son así en la vida real. La evasión, como

la corrupción, tiene un montón de costos económicos para
el sistema, además de los sociales y éticos, por supuesto."

As we have already seen, the history of human groups can be studied
in multiple contexts, and in any one of them the human being is divided
between the just and the unjust, the honest and the dishonest, the legal and
the illegal.

The perpetuation of the unjust, however, seems to demonstrate that
corruption accompanies man wherever he may or may not fight for survival.

Thomas Hobbes (2000: 255) has long asserted the importance of
combating corruption as a way of guaranteeing social peace:

> "Therefore the people must be taught to refrain from
> violence towards others by means of personal vengeance;
> of violation of marital honor; and of violent prey and
> fraudulent subtraction of each other's goods. For the
> purpose of which it is also necessary to be shown the bad
> consequences of false judgments, by corruption, or by
> judges, or witnesses, by which the distinction of property
> disappears and justice becomes of no effect."

By considering corruption as an irrefutable phenomenon within the
process of knowledge, Auguste Comte (2004: 110) stated:

> "Todo aquello que es positivo, es decir, basado en
> hechos bien constatados, es cierto: no hay posibilidad de
> distinción a este respecto. Parece evidente, en efecto, que
> antes de empezar el estudio metódico de alguna de las
> ciencias fundamentales, se debe estar preparado mediante
> el estudio de aquellas otras que traten de los fenómenos
> anteriores en nuestra escala enciclopédica, ya que estos
> influyen siempre de un modo decisivo sobre aquellos otros
> de los que nos proponemos conocer sus leyes."

The Organization of American States has been fully aware of the
danger posed by the misappropriation of public funds, which is why it has
issued the Inter-American Convention Against Corruption (IACAC). Its
preamble states:

"Los Estados miembros de la Organización de los Estados Americanos, CONVENCIDOS de que la corrupción socava la legitimidad de las instituciones públicas, atenta contra la sociedad, el orden moral y la justicia, así como contra el desarrollo integral de los pueblos;

CONSIDERANDO que la democracia representativa, condición indispensable para la estabilidad, la paz y el desarrollo de la región, por su naturaleza, exige combatir toda forma de corrupción en el ejercicio de las funciones públicas, así como los actos de corrupción específicamente vinculados con tal ejercicio;

PERSUADIDOS de que el combate contra la corrupción fortalece las instituciones democráticas, evita distorsiones de la economía, vicios en la gestión pública y el deterioro de la moral social;

RECONOCIENDO que, a menudo, la corrupción es uno de los instrumentos que utiliza la criminalidad organizada con la finalidad de materializar sus propósito;

CONVENCIDOS de la importancia de generar conciencia entre la población de los países de la región sobre la existencia y gravedad de este problema, así como de la necesidad de fortalecer la participación de la sociedad civil en la prevención y lucha contra la corrupción;"

Carlos A. Manfroni (2001: 20), in a comment to IACAC, lists seven reasons why corruption should be tackled internationally. They are:

"1) La corrupción es una materia demasiado sensible a los gobernantes, como para dejar a los gobernados indefensos frente al desinterés total de la comunidad internacional.

2) La apertura exige transparencia, como resguardo de la lealtad y la equidad en el intercambio económico entre las naciones.

3) Debe promoverse la paz y el desarrollo de los pueblos, hostigados por las cargas injustas derivadas de la corrupción, que a la vez constituye la excusa de los

grupos más violentos y sediciosos para atentar contra las instituciones.

4) El combate contra la corrupción es una manera de preservar la legitimidad de las instituciones y sistemas, que se ven socavados por una ilegitimidad de ejercicio, cuando no se gobierna para el bien común.

5) Es necesario combatir el crimen organizado y el narcotráfico, fin para el cual la cooperación internacional resulta imprescindible.

6) Hace falta una más amplia cooperación internacional para obtener información, pruebas y extradiciones.

7) Debe generarse mayor conciencia ética en la sociedad civil y un grado más alto de protección a las personas que tienen vocación y empeño para combatir la corrupción."

When quoting Tito Livio, Núñez (2006: 49) says that *Ninguna ley és cómoda para todos.*

We do not believe nor do we have the ambition of believing that the mere editing of laws on a national or international level solves problems of ethical or moral nature, yet we believe that the Rule of Law has an obligation to resist any kind of corruption with public resources, under penalty of losing the reason for existing.

# CHAPTER 8

# Is a Little of Corruption Necessary for the Development of Periphery Countries?

Ever since man became sedentary and realized that the riches of the Earth could give him a better life, he began to walk the path of income production.

It has been so with men and their associations in tribes, clans, cities, and finally, with the State, the greatest of all human association projects.

## 8.1 - Corruption and Rent-Seeking

Rent-seeking means more income and, therefore, better conditions to enjoy micro and macro social systems, which provide better health conditions, education, housing, safety, and leisure. The sum of these and other factors make up what the State calls dignity.

Rupert F. J. Pritzl (2006: 264-266) in his work *Corrupción y Rentismo en América Latina* notes that even though there are those who argue that rent-seeking produces social gains, it is proven that it generates negative effects that produce more social waste than social surplus. He says:

> "En su acepción más amplia, rentismo es el conjunto
> de posibilidades de obtener ingresos por la vía política,
> para los que JAGDISH BHAGWATI emplea también el
> término '*directly unproductive, profit-seeking (DUP)*

119

*activities'*. Las actividades de lobbyismo de los diferentes grupos no se agotan en generar ganancias y rentas monopólicas y abarcan todo otro tipo de transferencias de ingresos y privilegio otorgadas de parte del Estado y que surgen en el proceso político-burocrático soslayando o distorsionando el mercado económico. En tal sentido el término es abarcativo de variantes más específicas como

*'tariff— seeking', 'restriction-seeking', 'revenue seeking'* y *'premium seeking'."*

Pritzl was responsible for reproducing the distinction between the search for income and the search for usefulness in such a way that one can perceive hiding behind the rent-seeker a true utilitarian capable of imprisoning the State in order to obtain easy and fast profit.

In this way, he understands that the rent-seeking must be controlled so that it does not turn out to be another form of State takeover. Here is an excerpt that clarifies what Pritzl said (2006: 264-266,268):

"En un análisis macro, el *rent-seeking* o búsqueda de rentas, se distingue del *profit-seeking*, o búsqueda de utilidades, esencialmente en dos aspectos:

(1) En primer lugar, el rentismo no es una fuente de ingreso resultante de la actividad empresarial según SCHUMPETER (por ejemplo inversión de riesgo), sino una fuente de ingreso generada (en su mayor parte) artificialmente por injerencias del Estado en el proceso económico y una asignación política de recursos. De esta realidad derivan también los múltiples esfuerzos por ejercer influencia directa sobre la asignación de recursos y evitar que pueda establecerse una posible competencia.

(2) En segundo lugar, la lucha distributiva no se enciende en torno a las ganancias y los ingresos obtenidos en el mercado por los diferentes actores del juego social (empresarios y sindicatos); más bien se trata de distribuir posiciones de poder e influencia que garantizan a sus titulares una fuente de rentas segura y permanente. La búsqueda de utilidades, en cambio, consiste en tratar de

obtener ganancias temporarias que la competencia se encarga de corregir con el tiempo.

En términos generales, *rent-seeking* significa aprovechar oportunidades políticas de obtener ingresos a los efectos de apropiarse de rentas políticas con carácter permanente, mientras que el *profit-seeking* define los esfuerzos por obtener ingresos económicos que permiten obtener rentas económicas solamente temporales."

# 8.2 — Rent-Seeking and Rupture of the Principle of Equality

The utilitarian rent-seeking becomes a negative process because it promotes the rupture of the principle of equality in creating a cycle in which the fast and easy gain overcomes the production compromising the long-term development, as emphasized by Pritzl (2000:251,270):

"El dinero fluye hacia el poder. El poder permite generar ingresos, los ingresos acrecientan el poder. [Esta]... acumulación es mucho más atractiva que la acumulación que pueda obtenerse a partir de los medios de producción. (...)

La diferencia en la capacidad de organización y de presión de diferentes sectores suele llevar a una distribución desigual de ingresos y riquezas en donde prevalece el interés (1) de grupos minoritarios por sobre el interés de sectores populares, (2) el interés obtener ingresos por sobre el destino que se le dará a los ingresos y (3) el interés por defender los ingresos existentes por sobre la creación de nuevos ingresos."

# 8.3 — Legal Rent-Seeking and Illegal Rent-Seeking

Not all rent-seeking is illegal, as we have already mentioned, but even legal forms of rent-seeking may not be honest because *non omne quod licet honestum est* (not all that is permitted is honorable).

One needs to understand that whenever the law grants privileges to someone, it is necessarily diminishing the socioeconomic and legal share of another, and such an act implies a violation of the principle of equality.

Whenever a person uses the State to obtain personal benefits, he or she must be penalized for the practice of illegal rent-seeking, as Pritzl (2000: 291-292) points out:

> "En estas circunstancias, los políticos y la burocracia pueden aprovechar todo su poder para definir y aplicar los derechos de propiedad en beneficio propio. Los límites que se fijen dependerá solamente de su cálculo racional (asegurarse el poder) que no necesita respetar ningún tipo de condicionamientos institucionales secundarías.
>
> De lo señalado se desprende que la generalizada corrupción pública en muchos países del Tercer Mundo, debe ser interpretada análogamente como rentismo dinámico ilegal que distorsiona las estructuras de decisión al superponerle motivos ajenos a la función y modificar en el más largo plazo el marco de acción institucional. La conducta de los funcionarios ya no es guiada por la mejor solución técnica posible y, en cambio, prevalecen motivos personales de poder y enriquecimiento personal. (…)
>
> La utilización del Estado como forma de satisfacer intereses personales es uno de los principales problemas políticos en los países de— América Latina y en gran parte responsable por el inmovilismo social que se observa a nivel económico y social, la sostenida y gravosa desigualdad social y los avances relativamente modestos en materia de desarrollo. Por lo tanto, si no se revierte esta situación no cabe esperar un desarrollo económico sostenido en los países de América Latina."

# 8.4 - How Much Corruption is Necessary for the Development of Periphery or Developing Countries?

Illegal rent-seeking is one of the forms of corruption.

Juan Bautista Cincunegui and Juan de Dios Cincunegui (1996: 16), when writing about corruption and its factors of power, confirm the idea that it has no borders, it devastates the poor countries, and it is increasing at a fast pace among the wealthy nations, too:

> "El 'soborno' por parte de empresas de los países desarrollados se produciría en los países periféricos como única posibilidad de desarrollo económico, frente al sistema generalizado de corrupción de los mismos. Si bien Max Weber sostiene dicha teoría, Klitgaard afirma que"...hay pruebas de que ciertas formas de conductas corruptas están aumentando hoy en las naciones más avanzadas en lo económico y político" y cita escándalos de corrupción en los más altos niveles de gobierno de Holanda, Alemania, Gran Bretaña, Israel, Japón y Estados Unidos..."

Does the development of non-hegemonic countries need corruption as a kind of extra force for the implementation of public policies and services? Joseph La Palombara (198: 274-275), in his work *A Política no Interior das Nações*, states:

> "Corrupt forms of administration have, in the past, constituted important aspects of the implementation of public policy in nations, such as the United States and Great Britain, as they are, and today, in nations such as the Soviet Union and Israel. Depending on what a society wants to be done, corrupt behavior may appear to us as a sufficient, necessary, or acceptable condition for achieving goals. Objective cost-benefit analysis connected with purposes that are considered important to society

can easily lead us to the conclusion that corruption is an acceptable cost.

Some forms of corruption are so universal and seem an instinctive dimension of human interaction that looking for ways to eliminate them would be counterproductive. Experienced societies have already learned to close their eyes to such practices or to redefine them as non-corrupt. The Soviet mill manager who illegally accumulates stockpiles of scarce resources in strong demand may simply become a good 'entrepreneur,' who fully meets his production quotas in a timely manner. Bakchich in Asia, as proteksia in the Israeli administration, are relatively moderate forms of exchange of influence or of bribery, too ingrained to be eliminated. Trying to do so would certainly entail such high costs that would far outweigh the possible benefits of the measure. It is noteworthy that the Israeli word proteksia has been imported from Eastern Europe where the authorities have come to the conclusion that they cannot change the structural conditions that make corruption necessary in economic and social terms."

Corruption is the enemy of every form of State, but especially of substantial democracy because it bases its existence on the principle of just equality among the unequal. This means that inequalities are acceptable to the extent that they promote the common good and not personal benefit at the expense of the public treasury.

To say that a little corruption is necessary for the development of the peripheral countries because of the speed that bribery impinges on the negotiations is to bribe one's conscience, to subvert ethics, and to conform to the unjust.

Corruption in the form of utilitarian rent-seeking undermines the health of the public coffers and makes public policies a fallacy. It is our understanding that the corruption resulting from crimes against the public administration and from the misconduct of public officials represent an obstacle to the development and consolidation of substantial democracy, which is why the fight against corruption must be elevated to the category of public policy.

# 8.5 - The Perception of Corruption by the World Media

Perhaps there is not a single day when one or more cases of corruption with public money is released on the world media. Gail Russel Chaddok from the American newspaper *The Christian Science Monitor* and *La Prensa* said that *Los sobornos inflan el precio de contratos, desalientan las inversiones, y han aumentado en un tercio la deuda de los países pobres.*

Corruption impoverishes the countries where it is installed because it internally feeds from it.

The misappropriation of public funds represents the decrease in investment in social programs and requires the collection of more taxes and loans that fuel the increase of domestic and foreign debt, which in turn hinders development.

The press, through its investigative journalism, is also an instrument for controlling corruption, as we have already discussed in our book on Administrative Law.

In this scientific work, we avoid discussing specific cases of corruption due to the profusion with which they occur in Mercosur.

We have chosen a mission that we believe is more perennial, namely identifying causes, allies, effects, and pointing out instruments to fight corrupt practices that damage the effectiveness of public policies.

# 8.6 - The Perception of Corruption by the Third Sector

Transparency International (TI) defends that corruption is the abuse of entrusted power for private gain. This Civil Society Organization not only watches but also publishes the CPI – Corruption Perception Index - from almost two hundred countries, including countries members of the Mercosur.

It is important to emphasize the explanation of the Transparency International about the index it discloses:

"The Corruption Perception Index classifies countries
and territories according to the perceptions on the level

of corruption in the public sector. The study measures the level of perceived corruption using a scale of 0 (very corrupt) to 100 (completely clean)."

The organization clarifies that *El Índice de Percepción de la Corrupción (IPC) 2010 es un indicador compuesto que reúne datos de fuentes correspondientes a dos años anteriores. Para el IPC 2010, se incluyeron encuestas publicadas entre enero de 2009 y septiembre de 2010.*

According to the ranking of the 178 countries surveyed, Mercosur members appear in the following positions (note that the closer to 178th, the greater the perception of corruption by society). Here is the 2010 ranking:

- Argentina: 105
- Brazil: 69
- Paraguay: 146
- Uruguay: 24

The Corruption ranking in 2012 shows insignificant progress in Brazil and Argentina. It seems that only Uruguay continues to fight corruption with determination and interest to be seen as one of the least corrupt countries in the Americas. Venezuela, recently admitted as a member of Mercosur, is shamefully the ninth most corrupt country among the 174 investigated. Here is the 2012 ranking:

- Argentina: 102
- Brazil: 69
- Paraguay: 150
- Uruguay: 20
- Venezuela: 165

The Chilean organization *Latinobarómetro* published, in 2010, a study carried out in 18 countries demonstrating how corruption affects the levels of wealth and poverty. Here's an excerpt from what was released:

"On Monday, March 7[th,] at the headquarters of SEGIB, the director of the *Latinobarómetro*, Marta Lagos, presented the 2010 edition of this study, which annually applies about 19,000 interviews in 18 Latin American countries, representing more than 400 million inhabitants.

Only 16% of Latin Americans think that their country is safe; 31% believe that police corruption is the main obstacle to better safety, and they believe that it is necessary to increase the number of police officers.

After this, the economic problems of poverty and unemployment were analyzed, which are the main reasons for concern for 38% of citizens. Only 21% consider that the distribution of wealth is fair, and this indicator practically does not offer improvements over the years. About 39% consider that their country is progressing. 77% of citizens believe that democracy, despite presenting problems, is the best system of government. Also, 60% think that government decisions are taken to privilege minorities (in 2002, 72% had the same opinion)."

In December 2013, the numbers released by TI revealed that only Uruguay continues to advance in the fight against corruption. Here is the 2013 ranking:

- Argentina: 106
- Brazil: 72
- Paraguay: 150
- Uruguay: 19
- Venezuela: 160

We consider it important to say that countries that feel morally affected by the disclosure of Transparency International's Corruption Perceptions Index always try to invalidate it, either by criticizing the method or the way data was collected.

The citizen knows that there is no full accuracy in such data, but it is also a fact that no one doubts that the index is closer to reality than the official data. After all, it is enough to follow the indexes of the internal and external sectors that control the public sector, as well as the daily reports of the investigative journalism of each Mercosur member country to verify how corrupt the governments of the region are.

I wish Transparency International could change the term Corruption Perception Index to "Government Corruption Perception Index." I think it would better characterize it is not the Nation that is corrupt, but that small portion that holds power and which we call government.

# 8.7 - The Academic Perception of Corruption

Juan Carlos Ferré Olivé (2002: 20), Professor of Criminal Law at the University of Salamanca states:

> "La corrupción de funcionarios públicos y autoridades es uno de los grandes problemas de nuestro tiempo. Este fenómeno, que afecta por igual al mundo rico y al mundo pobre, genera para los responsables unos ingresos económicos extraordinarios, que necesariamente deben reincorporar al circuito económico 'legal' para su disfrute. Aquí es donde cobra especial trascendencia la figura penal del blanqueo de dinero. La corrupción es también un problema que la Comisión Europea quiere atacar con energía…"

A study carried out with the support of the University of Buenos Aires, the National Academy of Education, and the Ford Foundation (Chile), *Corrupción y Democracia en La Argentina: La interpretación de los estudiantes universitarios* (2005: 31) shows that the contamination of justice and the misappropriation of public funds account for 55% of the most serious consequences of corruption, according to the perception of Argentine university students, as shown in the following chart:

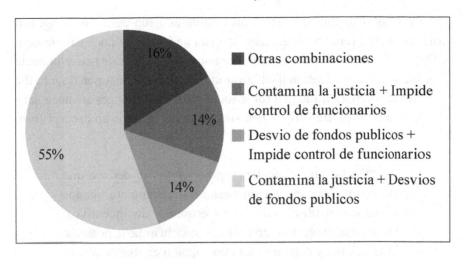

16%

14%

55%

14%

■ Otras combinaciones

■ Contamina la justicia + Impide control de funcionarios

■ Desvio de fondos publicos + Impide control de funcionarios

■ Contamina la justicia + Desvios de fondos publicos

Héctor A. Mairal (2007: 15-16), when studying the legal roots of corruption in Argentina, points out that:

"En la Argentina se tiene la percepción, apoyada en datos de la realidad y confirmada por encuestas nacionales e internacionales, que su difusión es muy alta, incluso en comparación con países vecinos y de similares características sociales, económicas y culturales: 'El fenómeno de la corrupción está masivamente generalizado en la sociedad argentina' (...) De acuerdo con una encuesta Gallup de 1996, el 97% del público del Gran Buenos Aires consideraba que el nivel de corrupción en Argentina es alto o muy alto, mientras que Transparency International colocaba a Argentina en el puesto 35 entre 54 países ordenados de menor a mayor según su nivel de corrupción, significativamente detrás de Chile (N° 21), resultado que se repetía en un índice preparado por la misma organización y en el cual con un índice de 3 para el año 1998 (de un máximo de 10 para los países en los que no se observan prácticas corruptas como ocurre con Nueva Zelanda), Argentina estaba detrás de Chile (6,8), Uruguay (4,3) y aun de Brasil (4). La percepción desde entonces no ha mejorado."

In a quest to find means of preventive and repressive fight against corruption and rent-seeking, Juan Bautista and Juan de Dios Cingunegui (1996: 16 17), in their work *La corrupción y los factores de poder* indicate that the social organization itself around institutions is an open door to the practice of corruption and that some socio-structural changes are necessary to create a kind of firewall against such practice. Here is an excerpt from what they say:

> "De las consideraciones precedentes se deduce que la corrupción y el rentismo están estrechamente ligados al marco institucional y a su esquema de incentivos. Siendo así, el objetivo consiste en modificar la disposición institucional y convertir a la corrupción en una conducta que deje de ser 'redituable' para los involucrados. De este modo, los potenciales infractores deberán descartarla como alternativa válida desde una perspectiva racional. (…)

En el orden político es indispensable introducir las siguientes transformaciones:

> — Democratización del sistema político: Una democratización del sistema político generaría una mayor participación popular en las decisiones y, al mismo tiempo, un mayor control de la gestión pública. La libertad política que se obtiene con una mayor democratización no sólo entraña un considerable valor social en sí mismo, sino que -desde una perspectiva instrumental— también sirve a la organización de una sociedad civil activa que controle la gestión pública. Una sociedad libre, constituida por seres humanos libres e iguales, probablemente sería inconcebible sin democracia, único sistema político que permite concretar la soberanía popular.

En tal sentido, el restablecimiento o la adopción de sistemas democráticos en casi todos los países de América Latina es un primer paso alentador. El siguiente paso debe consistir en medidas políticas que consoliden institucionalmente las reformas efectuadas y los resultados alcanzados. A raíz del riesgo que encierra un eventual retorno a regímenes autoritarios o de recaída en políticas populistas, no debe subestimarse la importancia de una consolidación institucional.

— Implementación del Estado de derecho: La plena vigencia de los principios de Estado de derecho y división de poderes contribuye a reducir la arbitrariedad en las acciones del Estado y, en consecuencia, incrementa el grado de seguridad jurídica en la sociedad. En este contexto cobra especial significado el requisito de una justicia independiente y de un equilibrio entre Poder Legislativo y Poder Ejecutivo.

— Descentralización de estructuras y decisiones públicas'. En vista de la gran cantidad de sistemas centralistas en América Latina (en su mayoría legados de la época colonial), es necesario impulsar una descentralización de las estructuras y decisiones públicas. Es fundamental que no sólo se constituyan estructuras y organismos administrativos descentralizados, sino que también se deleguen las funciones y las atribuciones en los organismos descentralizados. La descentralización institucional debe ir acompañada de una descentralización funcional. Una dosis mayor de subsidiariedad y federalismo contribuiría además a una división vertical de poderes y generaría una aproximación al ciudadano.

De este modo podría reducirse la brecha aparentemente insalvable entre las todopoderosas autoridades públicas y los indefensos ciudadanos.

— Ley de financiamiento de los partidos: Para lograr un adecuado funcionamiento del sistema democrático es esencial contar con una legislación unívoca y transparente que regule el accionar de los partidos políticos, especialmente su modo de financiamiento. En un sistema de competencia democrática los partidos políticos son estrictamente necesarios. Por ende, sus funciones y financiamiento deben ser regulados en forma clara y transparente.58 Un financiamiento según normas fijas y claras, dictadas por el Estado59, reduciría el uso indebido de la función pública para fines partidarios (por ejemplo, como método para compensar un insuficiente financiamiento).

— Control recíproco de los poderes: Destacado ya que una división institucional, personal y funcional entre los poderes Legislativo, Ejecutivo y Judicial generaría un mejor control recíproco. Esta separación constituye un elemento fundamental para todo Estado moderno y democrático. Además, a fin de mejorar el control de la gestión, se requiere tolerancia para respetar a la oposición política y para garantizar la existencia de una prensa libre e independiente.

En el orden económico son prioritarias las siguientes medidas:

— Introducción de estructuras de mercado: Es necesario acotar el intervencionismo estatal y liberalizar las estructuras económicas. Muchas medidas no sólo fueron innecesarias, sino que además resultaron contraproducentes, sin que se haya procedido a su derogación por los consabidos motivos ligados al enriquecimiento personal.

Hay ciertos elementos que indican que una mayor competencia en el orden político y económico contribuye a que los resultados del proceso se orienten hacia las preferencias de los ciudadanos (soberanía del electorado y de los consumidores) y que la competencia social contribuye a que surja un control 'desde abajo'. Tomando el criterio del economista ordoliberal FRANZ BÖHM, puede afirmarse que se trata de la única alternativa para que la competencia actúe como 'instrumento desarticulador de estructuras de poder económico' enquistadas en la sociedad. Coincidimos con ERNST DÜRR en recomendar la adopción de un régimen de 'economía social de mercado'.

Las medidas de liberalización, desregulación y privatización permiten modificar estructuras sociales básicas. La transformación debe reducir las chances de obtener ingresos políticos improductivos -como las que plantea la búsqueda de rentas—, reemplazándolas por formas de ingresos económicos productivos.

Es una exageración decir que las medidas de descentralización y privatización no hacen más que convertir la corrupción pública en privada, sin conseguir que disminuya la corrupción en su conjunto. La sucinta comparación de estructuras formulada en el capítulo 3 no sólo puso de manifiesto que la corrupción en el ámbito privado tiene una dimensión menor a la del sector público, sino que además demostró que su importancia cualitativa es considerablemente inferior.

La circunstancia conocida como 'paradoja de la privatización' señala que el proceso de privatización y venta de empresas públicas poco rentables se constituye en una fuente de corrupción y concentración de ingresos aún mayor, porque las empresas fueron vendidas 'por debajo de la mesa' a amigos o parientes. Sin embargo, este análisis soslaya el problema propiamente dicho. En efecto, el problema no radica en la privatización en sí, sino en comprender cómo aprovechan los funcionarios públicos el proceso privatizador para volcar las decisiones en beneficio propio, de amigos o parientes. Las condiciones de la privatización permiten que políticos y burócratas corruptos privilegien sus propios intereses desde el ejercicio de la función pública. Además, es importante que el proceso esté acompañado de medidas políticas y económicas complementarias, ya que de lo contrario se produciría un 'mero' traspaso, una 'privatización aparente'. Entre estas medidas adicionales podríamos mencionar: flexibilización de los precios, desregulación y apertura de los mercados y liberalización de toda la economía.

En un nivel más técnico de la administración es importante adoptar las siguientes medidas:

— Control más efectivo de la gestión administrativa: Si se reduce el margen de acción discrecional de los funcionarios públicos más encumbrados y se delimitan claramente las competencias y atribuciones, disminuirán también las posibilidades de que en el proceso de la toma de decisiones influyan consideraciones interesadas. Estos márgenes discrecionales y de decisión constituyen 'las puertas por las que penetra la corrupción Una mejora en la rendición de cuentas y en las auditorías debería contribuir a lograr un control externo más eficaz. Cabe esperar, por ejemplo, que en El Salvador se confirme esta hipótesis a partir de la reciente creación de la Corte de Cuentas. Evidentemente lo esencial es generar una reducción de los costos de información y control para terceros, de modo de facilitar el control interno y externo sobre la gestión de los funcionarios.

Una condición fundamental e indispensable para un control eficaz es que las instancias de contralor sean independientes. Como ya se ha dicho, en muchos países no se cumple este requisito. Esta circunstancia se puede verificar fácilmente en el caso de la justicia, que posee un estrecho vínculo con los responsables políticos y que suele presentar dependencias personales.

— Licitación pública: En lugar de una contratación directa basada en una decisión difícilmente controlable, sería recomendable la implementación de licitaciones públicas (si es posible, de carácter internacional). Aun cuando este mecanismo no es infalible para frenar la corrupción, ciertamente contribuye a hacer más transparentes y controlables las decisiones de la administración pública.

— Aumentos salariales en el sector público: Para reducir la necesidad de incurrir en actos de corrupción (sobre todo en los niveles inferiores de la administración pública) e incrementar la calidad y motivación de los empleados, sería conveniente elevar el nivel salarial en el sector público. Como en muchos casos existe un excedente de personal, sería necesario reducir simultáneamente la cantidad de funcionarios con lo cual se operaría una cierta compensación en la composición total del gasto.

Estas medidas en el nivel técnico administrativo apuntan sobre todo a reducir los costos de control para terceros (descriptos en el modelo Principal-agente-cliente), de modo de otorgar mayor transparencia a las decisiones del Estado.

El tratamiento exhaustivo de las falencias jurídicas en los países latinoamericanos puso de manifiesto la necesidad de implementar importantes reformas. Una de esas medidas podría ser la introducción del principio de oralidad en los juicios, además del principio de legalidad. A continuación enumeraremos brevemente algunas medidas para el ámbito de la justicia:

— Mejor control de los fallos de conciencia de los jueces: El registro sistemático y la publicación de todas las decisiones judiciales permitiría comparar las decisiones de conciencia de los jueces y hacerlas controlables incluso por instancias ajenas a las instituciones judiciales. Al mismo tiempo, una recopilación de este tipo podría ayudar a los propios magistrados en el proceso previo a sus decisiones.

— Introducción de la figura del testigo principal o clave (Kronzeuge): La introducción de la figura del testigo principal sería doblemente beneficiosa. Por un lado, quienes demuestren en forma fehaciente que están dispuestos a abandonar la corrupción practicada en el pasado, tendrían el aliciente de una disminución de la condena; por el otro, podrían tomar estado público informaciones internas más precisas acerca de la corrupción sistemática.

— Inversión de la carga de la prueba: Si se invierte la carga de la prueba, los acusados de corrupción quedan obligados a demostrar el origen legal de su patrimonio, en cuyo caso se simplifica y acelera el procedimiento contra los imputados. Sin embargo, tal como dijimos en un párrafo anterior, deben quedar excluidas meras 'denuncias de corrupción' planteadas por la opinión pública que en muchos casos son una forma concreta de hacer política y eliminar adversarios incómodos. Además hay que tener en cuenta que esta inversión de la carga de la prueba -y, del mismo modo, la introducción de la figura del testigo principal— debe regirse por los principios del Estado de derecho. Por lo tanto, es válido el principio según el cual toda persona deberá ser considerada inocente hasta tanto se demuestre lo contrario.

Incautar los beneficios procedentes de actos de corrupción no transgrede los principios del Estado de derecho. La incautación no sólo debe ser permitida por ley, sino aplicada efectivamente. Impedir una 'recompensa' institucional constituiría otro valioso aporte a la lucha contra la corrupción.

Ya hicimos referencia a la creación y difusión de escuelas para jueces en algunos países de América Latina. Las primeras experiencias obtenidas con estas instituciones que buscan mejorar la formación y capacitación de los magistrados han sido positivas.

— Reforma de los códigos penales: Otra contribución importante sería la de una reforma penal que permita definir con mayor precisión los hechos de la corrupción y su alcance, y que luego penalice más severamente este tipo de delito. El derecho penal ganaría en credibilidad y tendría un efecto disuasorio si se implementaran eficazmente los instrumentos legales y se aplicaran castigos más severos. Además sería conveniente que las modificaciones al Código Penal (interpretadas como recurso de última instancia) se produjeran luego de un profundo debate social sobre corrupción. (PRITZL, Rupert: Corrupción y Rentismo en América Latina. Buenos Aires: CIEDLA, Fundación Honrad Adenauer, 2000. p. 339, 341— 348.)

'Como dice Lipovetsky, "los ideales de bienestar, la pérdida de crédito de los grandes sistemas, la extensión de los deseos y derechos a la autonomía subjetiva, han vaciado de su substancia a los deberes cívicos al igual que han desvalorizado los imperativos categóricos de la moral individual e interindividual, en el lugar de la moral del civismo, tenemos el culto de la esfera privada y la indiferencia hacia la cosa pública, el dinero todopoderoso y la democratización de la corrupción". (...)

El "soborno" por parte de empresas de los países desarrollados se produciría en los países periféricos como única posibilidad de desarrollo económico, frente al sistema generalizado de corrupción de los mismos.

Si bien Max Weber sostiene dicha teoría, Klitgaard afirma que "... hay pruebas de que ciertas formas de conductas corruptas están aumentando hoy en las naciones más avanzadas en lo económico y político" y cita escándalos de corrupción en los más altos niveles de gobierno de Holanda, Alemania, Gran Bretaña, Israel, Japón y Estados Unidos. Podemos agregar otros como los escándalos de Italia ("mano pulite") o España (Guardia Nacional).

Se ha dicho que cuando mayor es la injerencia del Estado en la economía, mayor es la posibilidad de que se agudicen los procedimientos corruptos, dado que en la medida en que se requieran actos de la Administración para habilitaciones, inscripciones, controles, fijación de precios, otorgamiento de subsidios y privilegios, entre otros, mayor será la posibilidad de que la autorización gubernamental se produzca junto a un soborno y, viceversa, que se trabe el ingreso al mercado de competidores mediante el pago de dinero por la empresa ya instalada."

The roots of corruption identified by Héctor Mairal are based in Brazil and throughout Latin America. On the other hand, Mairal points out some solutions to strengthen our democratic state, which can be applied to any country in the world.

Here are some of his reflections:

1)  *the need for greater democratization of the political system with greater participation of popular control;*
2)  *more independence for justice and balance between the government branches;*
3)  *law that regulates the activities of political parties, especially, their funding;*

4) *restriction of State interventionism and liberalization of economic structures;*

5) *more effective control of the State administration and of public biddings;*

6) *to pay more fairly, and even, to increase pay to public servants as a way of combating corruption;*

7) *greater control of the judges' activities;*

8) *to give priority to the "key or main witness", that is, to promote plea bargaining;*

9) *to reverse the burden of proof, that is, to compel the corrupt with the burden of proving the origin of their assets;*

10) *reform of penal codes at the level of better defining or typifying acts of corruption.*

Based on the investigations that we have carried out in Mercosur and aware of the possible solutions, we try to take advantage of the present work to propose the unification of criminal, administrative, and administrative disciplinary legislation to fight against acts of corruption arising from misappropriation of public property, money, and income.

If there is a political-legal will to unify the legislation, as we have seen, Mercosur may become a model of effective fight against corruption and, certainly, a more pleasant place for its peoples.

# CHAPTER 9

# The State, Sovereignty, Formal Democracy and Its Crisis

The State as a conjunction of people, territory, and sovereign government is a recent institution in history. Formerly, one worked with the concept of "kingdom" or "empire". Later, the Greeks began to work with the concept of city-state. It is Cicero, the Roman statesman, that more than any other will work the concept of Republic.

It is an academic-legal consensus that the idea of State that we have today begins in the 17$^{th}$ century.

In order to arrive at the republican form, the representative system and the democratic regime of government, history has gone a long way in time.

Evolution has made man go through various forms of association: the family, the tribe, the kingdoms, the *polis*, the republic, and lastly, the greatest of them all, the democratic state.

In all forms of association with emphasis on governments that we have cited, there are records of some current administrative principles and political and legal institutes, such as:

1 - planning;
2 - coordination;
3 - control;
4 - decentralization;
5 - delegation of competence;
6 - hierarchy; and
7 - objective standards.

While in the evolutionary process common interests are the greatest amalgam of civilizations, corruption is the most disruptive factor in history.

In religion, the strongest govern with those of similar interest. In Darwinian evolutionism, the strongest go together, devouring the weakest in an infinite chain, as recalled by the CIA Report (2006: 35):

"The Darwinist conception is very strong in American society because it believes that the world has to be in the hands of the most qualified and endowed by God to exercise this leadership. Hegemony is not done with weakness, and power is what is not lacking for the USA, others like it or not."

When the man discovered that associating with other would bring more benefits than living alone, he sought to broaden his domains through exchange and other forms of alienation of goods.

From this historical journey and from this subjection of the environment to the interests of the sedentary man, the modern State is born, once the growth of this historical group made them think of inhabiting the same territory and of extracting its provisions. This is how the State will protrude in time and space and print its ideological bias of power and domination.

Men with culture and common territory tend to rationalize their existence and functions as a society.

This is how the man organized himself into a state political body, not unlike what he already knew in the family, the tribe, and the *polis*. He conquered and divided power, and this is how the State has been formed under the sign of the promise of freedom, equality, and fraternity.

These promises are still the social amalgam, as Nietzsche (2007: 61) states:

> "Criar un animal al que le "sea posible hacer promesas", ¿No es, precisamente, esta misma paradójica tarea la que la naturaleza se ha propuesto con respecto al hombre?"

Social groups were formed by biological lineage, by cultural affinity, and, above all, by common interests. However, once associated, the prosperity of some has aroused the greed of others, and the unprofitable accumulation of wealth has generated the social imbalance we know of.

Engels (vol.2: 175) has mastered on the subject, by saying:

"The distinction of rich and poor appears beside that of freemen and slaves - with the new division of labor, a new cleavage of society into classes. (...)Their neighbors' wealth excites the greed of peoples who already see in the acquisition of wealth one of the main aims of life. They are barbarians: they think it more easy *(sic)* and in fact more honorable to get riches by pillage than by work."

This moment of evolution over which there is no known historical landmark has awakened in man the need to proclaim sovereignty over a geographical territory as a warning to other groups that such territory would be his wealth and where he would exercise his power against external aggressions. From this historical moment, the ruling class and the dominated class emerge, as Engels implies (vol.2: 121):

"But the Athenians were soon to learn how rapidly the product asserts its mastery over the producer when once exchange between individuals has begun and products have been transformed into commodities. With the coming of commodity production, individuals began to cultivate the soil on their own account, which soon led to individual ownership of land. Money followed, the general commodity with which all others were exchangeable. However, when men invented money, they did not think that they were again creating a new social power, the one general power before which the whole of society must bow. And it was this new power, suddenly sprung to life without knowledge or will of its creators, which now, in all the brutality of its youth, gave the Athenians the first taste of its might."

Once again, Engels (vol.2: 181), when writing about the emergence of the State, says:

"The state is therefore by no means a power imposed from outside to society; just as little is it "the reality of the moral idea," "the image and the reality of reason," as Hegel maintains. Rather, it is a product of society at a particular stage of development; it is the admission that this society has involved itself in insoluble self-contradiction and is cleft into irreconcilable antagonisms which it is powerless to exorcise. But in order that these antagonisms, classes with conflicting economic interests, shall not consume themselves and society in fruitless struggle, a power, apparently standing above society, has become necessary to moderate the conflict and keep it within the bounds of "order"; and this power, arisen out of society, but placing itself above it and increasingly alienating itself from it, is the state."

Man continues to build a history of associationism and dependence, sacralizing life and giving up full freedom to enable and strengthen the emergence of institutions such as the State.

Part of this reflection is found when Claudio Araujo Reis (2005: 322-323) says:

"Man's relationship to things is already a relationship of dependence. The idea of dependence is inseparable from the idea of this relationship to things. But, as we have seen, this relationship, which is absolutely devoid of moral value, does not add much to the way one thinks about man. The more complex model of needs, which implies needs to be met, call for cooperation, division of labor and exchange, introduces, as has already been seen previously, a new type of dependency: through the network of relationships originated by cooperation, individuals are no longer dependent on things alone, but also on each other. This dependence is still not especially problematic if it is seen only under the idea of utility: in this case, there would not be a particularly significant difference between depending on an automaton or depending on another man (understood to be dependent on his work) to have your needs met. The problem of dependence arises when one considers oneself under the concept of authority. Unlike the relationship of utility, which contains only, as in germ, some characteristic elements of moral relationship fully developed, the relationship of authority, essentially defines itself as a relationship between wills, is clearly in the moral domain. Rousseau has already been seen as affirming that is not authority, but freedom, the greatest of all goods (cf. OC IV, 309). This dependence, that is, dependence on a will different from his own will, or submission to another will, is essentially 'disorderly.' "C'est par elle", he continues saying, "que le maitre et l' escave se dépravent mutuellement' (OC IV, 311). It is to solve the problem of authority, that is, of the ordering of particular wills, that Rousseau thinks the central artifice of the social pact."

Contrasting the emergence of the modern State with the Right of the People, Julio Barboza (1999: 23,176) affirmed in *Derecho Internacional Público:*

"se suele comenzar La historia Del derecho de gentes a partir de La paz de Westfalia de 1648 (Tratados de Munster y de Osnabruck), que puso fin a la Guerra de Treinta años. Es un punto de partida conveniente, porque a partir de ella comienza a generalizarse el sistema de Estados en Europa, y como vimos antes, El Estado es el factor más importante en la formación y aplicación del derecho internacional." (...) La creación de un nuevo Estado se produce cuando tienen lugar ciertos hechos: una comunidad, establecida en un cierto territorio y con un gobierno efectivo e independiente, aspira a ser reconocida como Estado Miembro de la comunidad internacional. Los demás Estados deberán comprobar si efectivamente tales hechos tienen existencia real. Puede también suceder que el Estado que busca reconocimiento a un antiguo Estado que perdió su independencia, como los países bálticos anexados a la URSS como consecuencia del pacto Ribbentrop-Molotov. Por declaración del 27/8/91, los miembros de la Comunidad Europea acogen calurosamente la restauración de la soberanía e independencia y conforman su decisión de establecer sin demora relaciones diplomáticas con ellos."

Friedrich Nietzsche (2007: 40), one of the fiercest critics of the State says that it is a big lie. He affirms:

"Estado se llama el más frío de todos los monstruos fríos. Es frío incluso cuando miente; y ésta es la mentira que se desliza de su boca: «Yo, el Estado, soy el pueblo.» ¡Es mentira!."

Nietzsche says so because he knows that from ever since every form of god has relegated man to eternally wait for better days, as portrayed in Homer (2007: 20) when Telemachus replies:

"Mother, why do you grudge our own dear minstrel joy of song, wherever his thought may lead? Don't blame the minstrel, blame Zeus, who makes men work hard for their living, and then gives them just what he chooses for each."

The objective conception of International Law says that the State is constituted by the union of people, territory, and a sovereign government. Quentin Skinner (2006: 10) in his book *The Foundations of Modern Political Thought* says:

"I consider, therefore, that my central thesis is confirmed by the fact that at the end of the sixteenth century, at least in England and France, we find the words State and État beginning to be used in the sense that they will have in modernity."

On virtue and corruption in civic life, Skinner (2006: 66) makes the following reflection:

"Namely, how to achieve such unity between the interests of the city and those of its citizens as individuals. To this question, the authors we are considering propose a response that, once developed by the Italian Renaissance humanists, would provide the foundations for one of the great intellectual traditions of analysis of virtue and corruption in civic life. We can say that, in the evolution of the modern political theory, there were two main lines of approach of this theme. One of them says that government will be effective whenever its institutions are strong, and corrupt whenever its machinery fails to function properly. (The great exponent of this conception is Hume.) The other line, on the other hand, is that if the men who control government institutions are corrupt, the best possible institutions will not be able to mold or restrain them, whereas, if they are virtuous, the quality of institutions will become a minor topic. This tradition, of which Machiavelli and Montesquieu are the greatest representatives, proclaims that it is not so much the machinery of government, but the very spirit of rulers, of the people, and of the laws that most need to be defended."

Arturo Fernández (2000: 91) when writing about the renewal of the notion of State mentions:

"Por otra parte la sociedad está cada vez más polarizada y sus disparidades sean sociales, regionales o intra-estatales, de mantenerse las actuales tendencias, pasarán de lo injusto a lo inhumano y quizás a lo inviable respecto a hacer más o menos posible la justicia y la libertad. Se ha producido una redefinición de los conceptos de trabajo, de empleo y de lugares de trabajo, cuyas consecuencias son, a nivel universal, altas tasas de desempleo y también altas tasas de empleo precario o precarizado, condiciones salariales extremadamente bajas y un grado de desprotección social creciente que es muy desparejo en el mundo y de acuerdo a los Estados. Esto ha conducido a una gran heterogeneidad social y a una atomización o fragmentación que destacan muchos sociólogos y observadores de la realidad mundial."

145

# 9.1 — National Sovereignty

Sovereignty is the power over which there is no other.

When the man migrated from nomadism to sedentary life and dazzled with the capacity for subsistence in the territory he chose to live, he began to worry about defending it.

Population growth, increased internal demands, the possibility of expanding the domain with the exchange and then the sale of goods, made man wish for the annexation of neighboring territory, installing fear and promoting the declaration of sovereignty in a kind of domino effect.

Only time has relativized this desire for absolute sovereignty because it has made man see that the neighbor is not always an enemy. He can even be a partner in the development process. Julio Barboza (1999: 25) says:

> "El principio más importante que se afirma en este primer período, que continuará algo relativizado, hasta nuestros días, es de la soberanía del Estado, esto es, que no hay sobre los Estados que componen la comunidad internacional forma alguna de poder superior. En él se inspira todo el derecho internacional llamado "clásico" y, con su naturaleza relativa, también el derecho actual."

Evolution has brought us into the republican form, the representative system, and the democratic regime of government foreseen in the overwhelming majority of modern constitutions, including in the Mercosur countries.

In Brazil, for example, the Federal Constitution of October 5th, 1988 ensures:

> "Article 1. The Federative Republic of Brazil, formed by the indissoluble union of the states and municipalities and of the Federal District, is a legal democratic state and is founded on:
>
> I – sovereignty; (...)
>
> Sole paragraph. All power emanates from the people, who exercise it by means of elected representatives or directly, as provided by this Constitution.

(...)

Article 34. The Union shall not intervene in the states or in the Federal District, except:

(...)

VII – to ensure compliance with the following constitutional principles:

a) republican form, representative system and democratic regime;

(...)

Article 5. All persons are equal before the law, without any distinction whatsoever, Brazilians and foreigners residing in the country being ensured of inviolability of the right to life, to liberty, to equality, to security and to property, on the following terms:

(...)

Paragraph 3. International human rights treaties and conventions which are approved in each House of the National Congress, in two rounds of voting, by three fifths of the votes of the respective members shall be equivalent to constitutional amendments.

Paragraph 4. Brazil accepts the jurisdiction of an International Criminal Court to whose creation it has expressed its adhesion."

The Constitution organizes and distributes State power, but it is from the proclamation and recognition of sovereignty that politically and legally the national power becomes effective.

When this same Constitution (the power of the powers) admits that the country can submit to a supranational order it expresses that it adopted the relative sovereignty as principle or foundation.

The first desire of the peoples seems to have been that of an absolute sovereignty, after all, fulfilling a dream exceeds its fruition, until time accommodates the thought.

With time and the advance of economic and telematic globalization, the concept of absolute sovereignty has become more and more relativized. Behold, the problems of a State can trigger reactions in distant markets.

The phase of absolute sovereignty has produced exacerbated patriotism, which isolates the State on an island under the pretense of safeguarding it from alien cultural, economic, or political influences. Norman Angell (2002: 176) said:

> "William Lecky, the author who has possibly written more lucidly about the suppression of religious persecution, observes that, although often presided over by a disinterested, high-minded person (for he denies the motive of interest in the persecutors), the struggle between opposing religious factions had not been purified by rationalism. And he adds that irrationality, which once characterized religious sentiment, has now been replaced by the irrationality of patriotism.

Lecky says:

> "If we take a sufficiently broad look at the course of history and examine the relations of the great human groupings, we find that religion and patriotism are the principal moral forces to which they have been subjected, and it can almost be said that particular modifications and reciprocal actions of these two agents constitute the moral history of humanity."

The twenty-first century demands that we rethink conceptions that time has worn. The concept of sovereignty, for example, has undergone mutations in International Law, specifically in Community Law dealing with consensual delegations of competence between sovereign States, and this way, in Community Law, States are subject to certain rules because they transferred partially certain attributions arising from sovereignty for the entity that groups them together.

The old format of sovereignty needs to be rethought as a concept and as a condition of coexistence between States in this new globalized world. Possessing land does not confer power like it used to do. Exploiting the land in a sustainable way and producing substantial equality is what confers sovereignty to a Nation.

I echo the voices that say that the modern State is in crisis and it needs to be rethought, as Manuel Hespanha (2005: 459) points out:

"Under our eyes, the State institution, as it had been constructed by liberal political theory, will dissolve and disappear. And with it, a series of exemplary models of living politics or having contact with power (suffrage, political parties, law, official justice). Even the imaginary linked to the State paradigm is in crisis: equality, as a political objective, is confronted with the pretensions of guarantee of difference; the general interest tends to yield to corporate or particularist claims; centralism is debated with all kinds of regionalism; the rule of law is attacked both in the name of the irreducibility of each case and of the judge's freedom of appreciation attached to it, as well as in the name of the ideas of conciliation and negotiation which make the law increasingly a contract between States and private groups; the "rationalizing" intention capitulates before the more radical liberal pretensions. The State itself, in the face of crisis of efficiency and legitimacy, seems to be incapable of, does not need, and does not want to maintain its orderly mission. In short, the State gradually abandons the political imaginary.

This state model had been designed according to a precise architecture, which foresaw:

(i) the strict separation between "political society" (the *polis*, i.e., the State and its institutions with *imperium*) and "civil society" (daily life and its "private" contractual arrangements of power) ;

(ii) distinction of the nature of powers, depending on whether they are powers of the State (public authorities) or powers of private ownership (private powers);

(iii) the establishment of a series of mediation mechanisms, based on the concept of "representation" (conceived as a product of the will, established by contract [term]), through which citizens living in civil society participated in the political society;

(iv) the identification of rights with the law, conceived as expressing the general will of the citizens, whose embodiment was the State;

(v) the institution of official justice, as the only instance of conflict resolution.

From the political point of view, this model, with the political consequences that it entails, promotes no enthusiasm whatsoever. However, the crisis is not just institutional, it is also a crisis of confidence on the part of citizens in legal and judicial institutions (crisis of "legitimacy"). Citizens not only ignore the law as much as they do not recognize it, that is, they do not recognize it as a suitable means of achieving their ideals of social organization or conflict resolution. The laws and regulations elaborated by a political world increasingly closed in itself, involved in a technicist and hermetic language, constituting an immense and impossible world to embrace, appear as a meaningless normative universe, far from the real problems of the people, monopolized by a group of beginners, suspected of protecting unspeakable interests. As for justice, its slowness, its price, and the impenetrability of its language have made the use of courts an expensive game with random results.

The proposal of alternative forms of law and justice is based precisely on these symptoms of crisis and it looks for other more effective and more acceptable ways of establishing norms of behavior and resolving conflicts.

In terms of establishing standards of behavior, there have been several proposals.

For some, the regulation of the State should be replaced by private initiative."

Rethinking the State means rethinking its corollaries. The legal positivism that has spread over the planet since the beginning of the last century, for example, does not enjoy the same prestige.

Contemporary man already knows that the raw law does not satisfy ones hunger for justice anymore and that there is much more promise in it than dignity or substantial citizenship.

The State and its substrates, especially the old principle of legality and legal equality, more and more resemble the literary fable classic opening statement "once upon a time..."

Rationalizing this new human awakening to the abstract thinking of the law and the substantiality of justice, Hespanha (2005: 466-467) points out:

> "Thus, there are several meanings of contemporary anti-legalism.
>
> The first is to refuse the will of the State - whatever it may be - inability to define criteria of justice and, therefore, to establish, absolutely and without appeal, the contents of the law. This orientation is no more than an update of an ever-recent theme in the history of European law - the theme of the existence of a natural right, unavailable to and therefore superior to political powers. However, it gained a new vigor at a time when the pretensions of State regulation were extended more than ever, having reached, with the twentieth-century totalitarianism (Nazism, Fascism, Stalinism), the end of a purpose to regulate life totally. Faced with these extreme forms of legalism, the concern to establish limits - formal (i.e., reservations of freedom) or material (i.e., non-derogable normative principles) - to State activity becomes much more imperative. They may be affiliated in this sense with anti-legalism, varied philosophical methodological orientations."

Perhaps this new way of rethinking the State is leading us more and more to a relative sovereignty in which it is important to live in harmony with the neighbors and where all take care of all, a formula that can make the development be distributed in a more equitable way.

I would insist that the European Union's attitude towards the Eurozone crisis in 2011 was a demonstration of this shared sovereignty by helping the countries in its zone of influence, for by allowing the "bankruptcy of Greece" and other countries in extreme difficulty economic crisis can represent chaos for rich countries and the threat that the poor will fall upon them.

Relief provided cannot mean the lack of accountability of inefficient public managers.

# 9.2 — Crisis in Democracy

Fred R. Dallmayr (2000: 33), in addressing the loss of importance of the State as the alpha and omega of political life, questions:

> "What are the theoretical and practical consequences, from the growing importance of the public sphere in various modern societies, of the relative loss of importance of the conception of the state as the alpha and omega of political life? Then to affirm that 'It is indispensable to develop a theory of the subject as a decentralized, incomplete agent, a subject built at the point of intersection of a multiplicity of subject positions, between which there is no *a priori* or necessary relation... what emerges are entirely new perspectives for political action, which neither liberalism, with its idea of the individual that only seeks its own interest, nor Marxism, with its reduction of all the positions of the subject to the class, can sanction and much less imagine."

Let us begin by recalling that democracy is a Greek conception, whose modern meaning was given by Abraham Lincoln in his well-known address at the Gettysburg Cemetery at the end of the war between the Union and the Confederate States of North America; that the French Revolution exposed the dream of freedom, equality, and fraternity; that the wars and especially State corruption have prevented a substantial democracy.

Professor Joseph La Palombara (1982: 56), when analyzing the crisis of the construction of Nations, states:

> "For one of the strangest characteristics of man is the excessive period of time during which he is able to withstand corruption, arbitrariness, and even political tyranny without protest and without active opposition."

In fact, there is no democracy without institutions legitimized by the people. The longevity of democracy as a government regime may perhaps be credited to the confidence that the people placed in State institutions, especially by the promise that they are the driving force of justice, equality, and unity among the interests of citizens. On the importance of the institutions, Skinner (2006: 66) is incontestable to the statement:

"We can say that, in the evolution of the modern political theory, there were two main lines of approach of this theme. One of them says that government will be effective whenever its institutions are strong, and corrupt whenever its machinery fails to function properly. (The great exponent of this conception is Hume.) The other line, on the other hand, understands that if the men who control government institutions are corrupt, the best possible institutions will not be able to mold or restrain them, while, if they are virtuous, the quality of institutions will become a minor topic. This tradition, of which Machiavelli and Montesquieu are the greatest representatives, proclaims that it is not so much the machinery of government, but the very spirit of the rulers, of the people, and of the laws that needs to be defended the most."

The crisis of the democratic system is due to the lack of implementation of its major promises, that is, the promotion of freedom, equality, and substantial fraternity. Quoting Ferrajoli, David Baigun (2006: 118-119) says:

"La crisis del sistema democrático, fue abordado por numerosos autores. Podemos señalar a Ferrajoli quien diferencia a la democracia sustancial o social y la formal o política, relacionando a la primera al 'estado de derecho', dotado de garantías efectivas, tanto liberales como sociales, y a la segunda con el 'estado político representativo', basado en el principio de mayoría como fuente de legalidad. Carlos Strasser hace referencia a la democracia limitada en función de su precariedad que son sus condiciones de posibilidad. Refiere, en este sentido, que 'fuera de los países más desarrollados muy grandes sectores de la población apenas tienen una condición ciudadana auténtica, es decir, en términos políticos de verdad democráticos se encuentran discapacitados, no gozan de la cantidad y calidad de educación, información, autonomía mínima, etc., necesarias'

La precariedad a la que hace referencia el autor citado en el párrafo que antecede, la podemos observar a partir de un informe de la CEPAL acerca de la realidad en América:

- El 44% de la población es pobre (25 millones).
- 100 millones de personas son indigentes.
- El 20% de la población más pobre obtiene el 3% del PBI.
- El 20% de la población más rica tiene el 58% del PBI.
- 74 millones de personas no tienen agua potable (14% de la población).
- La población en 1990 era de 129 millones de personas calculándose que para el 2015 será de 1033 millones."

Rupert Pritzl (2000: 53-54) states that the greatest threat to democracy is corruption.

"No se trata de defender el relativismo cultural, apoyado sobre todo en la década del '60 y que aún cuenta con algunos adeptos. Lo que se intenta es destacar la diferencia cualitativa, y en consecuencia cuantitativa, que indica que en sistemas políticos democráticos, la corrupción es un elemento político extraño y al mismo tiempo -según interpreta THALHEIM - destructivo para el sistema; mientras tanto, en los sistemas autoritarios o autocráticos, llega a constituirse en un elemento inherente al sistema e incluso actúa como estabilizador. A raíz de las diferentes formas de funcionamiento de los sistemas democráticos y autocráticos, la corrupción como recurso político siempre deberá interpretarse dentro del respectivo contexto.

Haciendo mención a NEIL SMELSER, representante de la teoría sociológica estructural-funcionalista, los politólogos ULRICH VON ALE— MANN y RALF KLEINFELD definen a la corrupción como a una determinada forma de imponer intereses particulares en el proceso político. De todos modos, siempre será necesario considerar el tipo de sistema político ante cuyo telón de fondo debe interpretarse esta 'especial forma de influencia política'. GUY KIRSCH señala al respecto:

'Lo que en la dictadura constituye una regla, en la democracia es una lamentable excepción. También se demuestra que lo que en una democracia constituye la regla, en la dictadura continúa siendo una excepción extraña al sistema.'"

In fact, the democratic state is neither as democratic as it seems to be nor is the law as fair as it is believed to be. However, between any form of absolutism and the least popular participation, Aristotle's thought remains alive when he said that democracy is the least of all possible evils.

Manuel Villoria Mendieta (2000: 67-68), in his work *Ética pública y corrupción*, points out 10 reasons why democracy is so desirable:

"En resumen, consideramos la democracia, con todos los requisitos antes esbozados, como la forma de gobierno legítima racional y moralmente. Dahl nos resume en diez las razones de su superioridad: 1. La democracia ayuda a evitar el gobierno de autócratas crueles y depravados. 2. La democracia garantiza a sus ciudadanos una cantidad de derechos fundamentales que los gobiernos no democráticos no garantizan ni pueden garantizar. 3. La democracia asegura a sus ciudadanos un ámbito de libertad personal mayor que cualquier alternativa factible a la misma. 4. La democracia ayuda a las personas a proteger sus propios intereses fundamentales. 5. Sólo un gobierno democrático puede proporcionar una oportunidad máxima para que las personas ejerciten su libertad de auto determinarse, es decir, que vivan bajo las leyes de su propia elección. 6. Solamente un gobierno democrático puede proporcionar una oportunidad máxima para ejercer la responsabilidad moral. 7. La democracia promueve el desarrollo humano más plenamente que cualquier alternativa factible. 8. Sólo un gobierno democrático puede fomentar un grado relativamente alto de igualdad política. 9. Las democracias representativas modernas no se hacen la guerra entre sí. 10. Los países con gobiernos democráticos tienden a ser más prósperos que los países con gobiernos no democráticos (1999, p. 72). La conclusión, consecuente con lo anteriormente expresado, es que la democracia, tal y como la definen los politólogos escogidos en el texto, ofrece más razones que ninguna otra forma de gobierno para ser aceptada y, por ello, establece el umbral de legitimidad mínimo, por debajo del cual todo otro régimen es ilegítimo."

On the other hand, Gabriel Andriasola (1999: 79), in his work *Delitos de corrupción pública,* when analyzing the correlation between corruption and democracy, says:

"Pero no es posible afirmar que la democracia es un antídoto siempre eficaz contra la corrupción. Sería deseable poder aseverarlo, pero la historia enseña que la corrupción puede llegar a constituir una enfermedad de la democracia. Los desbordes conocidos al final de la Revolución Francesa, las dificultades actuales de las antiguas democracias populares y los excesos de ciertos dirigentes en las democracias reinstaladas en América Latina, conducen a la prudencia. Incluso las democracias que mejor funcionan no están al abrigo de estos síntomas de crisis de la moral pública. No obstante, una democracia bien concebida y practicada, dotada de equilibrio a través de un sistema de frenos, contrapesos, contrapoderes y controles independientes, fundada en una moral de honestidad colectiva enseñada desde la escuela, administrada conforme a los principios de la transparencia de la publicidad y de la motivación de los actos públicos, es el régimen político más apto para luchar contra la corrupción. Pero solamente al precio de una gran vigilancia cotidiana de todas las fuerzas sociales la democracia puede luchar con éxito contra la corrupción."

# 9.3 - "He steals, but he delivers"- A Study by the University of Gothenburg in Sweden

Peter Esaiasson and Jordi Muñoz of the Department of Political Science at the University of Gothenburg, Sweden, conducted a study on the effects of "he steals, but he delivers" in Sweden (a country with a low incidence of corruption) and Spain (a country of average incidence of corruption) by comparing the perception of the population about the hypothesis of corruption versus competence of politicians who steal but deliver services to the population that elects them.

In 2007, the two researchers piloted a study in a small municipality in the Spanish autonomous community of Valencia, called Vall d'Alba, where Mayor Francisco Martinez was involved in an alleged corruption scandal accused of illegally earning thirteen real estate properties.

After modifying the qualification of the soil from agricultural to residential and industrial, the mayor sold some of these properties for prices higher than market value. In parallel to the belief that he was enriching with public money, he attracted investments to the municipality as it had never happened before. He gave the population a school, a medical center, a chapel, an industrial area, an indoor swimming pool, an elderly care center, a new police station, and even a bullfighting arena. Naturally, such feat raised political support in the following election to a staggering 71 percent in his favor.

Peter and Jordi's research uses the question "Why do voters often forgive corrupt politicians?" and analyzes the response given that says this occurs "because they deliver public services," noting that in the scientific literature this response is linked to "competence-corruption trade-off hypothesis", a study originally conducted by Rundquist and his colleagues in the 1970s (1977). It is the case of "competence versus corruption", where a corrupt politician has voting intention because of his competence.

Outside the academic world, the study embodies the Latin American saying *"roba pero hace"*, also a very popular expression and tradition in Brazil. The poll points to voters' preference for high-performing but corrupt politicians.

In 2013, two other researchers, Winters and Weitz-Shapiro, during a study done about the competence-corruption hypothesis in Brazil, considered a context of high corruption. The study failed to corroborate the hypothesis, despite the carefully designed experiment since they found little evidence that Brazilian voters are willing to ignore corruption in exchange for public services when they are given specific information about the corrupt behavior of the candidates.

Still in 2013, researchers Klasjna and Tucker working on the same hypothesis competence versus corruption in Sweden (considered a country of low corruption) and Moldova (considered highly corrupt) found that Moldovan voters were willing to support corrupt politicians when the economic conditions were good.

The studies also point that citizens who have assimilated the idea of "steals, but delivers" philosophically reduce the tension associated with voting for a corrupt but efficient politician. In such cases, when confronted with the fact that their candidates have committed an act of corruption, such voters minimize the severity of the offense by reason of the "he steals, but he delivers."

In the end, the researchers concluded that under certain conditions voters in the Organization for Economic Co-operation and Development (OECD) countries prefer to support candidates of their own choosing even when they are corrupt, as long as they are competent.

According to competence-corruption trade-off hypothesis, the results of the survey were surprising, pointing out that both in Sweden and in Spain voters prefer to support corrupt, but competent candidates, instead of honest but incompetent ones.

The researchers' biggest surprise was to note that even among Brazilian voters of the lower economic classes, "steals, but delivers" is no longer an option, as the studies of Winters and Weitz-Shapiro, conducted in 2013, show that Brazilian voters prefer an honest candidate, even with a poor performance, than a competent corrupt.

It is possible that this change is linked to the avalanche of cases of corruption that routinely plagues Brazil. It is a breath of fresh air to see that the resistance has begun…

# BOOK II

# Final Considerations

Obviously proposing the end of corruption would be the same as proposing the annihilation of the human race, reason why we would like to propose its reduction to tolerable levels.

We believe that the reduction on the levels of corruption depends on the sedimentation of democracy and the rule of law, since the formal democracy in which we live is producing resentments that will eventually require the exercise of the Right of Resistance by the Nation, as set forth in the Virginia Declaration of Rights, of June 12th, 1776, in its Article 3, *that government is, or ought to be, instituted for the common benefit, protection, and security of the people, nation, or community; of all the various modes and forms of government, that is best which is capable of producing the greatest degree of happiness and safety and is most effectually secured against the danger of maladministration.*

Modern constitutions, including the ones from the Mercosur countries, also bring the idea of impeachment as a political process of dismissal of the heads of the corrupt Executive Branch, as exemplified by the following articles of the 1988 Brazilian Constitution:

> *Article 85. Those acts of the President of the Republic which attempt on the Federal Constitution and especially on the following, are crimes of malversation:*
>
> I— *the existence of the Union;*
> II— *the free exercise of the Legislative Power, the Judicial Power, the Public Prosecution and the constitutional Powers of the units of the Federation;*

III— *the exercise of political, individual and social rights; IV – the internal security of the country;*

IV— *probity in the administration;*

V— *the budgetary law;*

VI— *compliance with the laws and with court decisions.*

*Sole paragraph. These crimes shall be defined in a special law, which shall establish the rules of procedure and trial.*

*Article 86. If charges against the President of the Republic are accepted by two thirds of the Chamber of Deputies, he shall be submitted to trial before the Supreme Federal Court for common criminal offenses or before the Federal Senate for crimes of malversation.*

*Paragraph 1. The President shall be suspended from his functions:*

*I – in common criminal offenses, if the accusation or the complaint is received by the Federal Supreme Court;*

*II – in the event of crimes of malversation, after the proceeding is instituted by the Federal Senate.*

*Paragraph 2. If, after a period of one hundred and eighty days, the trial has not been concluded, the suspension of the President shall cease without prejudice to the normal progress of the proceeding.*

*Paragraph 3. In the event of common offenses, the President of the Republic shall not be subject to arrest as long as no sentence is rendered.*

*Paragraph 4. During his term of office, the President of the Republic may not be held liable to acts outside the performance of his functions.*

The right of resistance is one of the ways in which we can evolve from the democratic state of law, in which empty promises of social dignity prevail, to realities in which democracies are substantial, that is, to safeguard at least a minimum of social dignity.

Printed in the United States
By Bookmasters